Together at Mass

WITH 24 LITURGIES OF THE WORD

Eugene S. Geissler

and

Kenneth W. Peters

AVE MARIA PRESS
Notre Dame, Indiana 46556

Nihil Obstat: John L. Reedy, C.S.C.
          Censor Deputatus

Imprimatur: Most Rev. Leo A. Pursley, D.D.
             Bishop of Fort Wayne/South Bend

© 1973 by Ave Maria Press. All rights reserved

Library of Congress Catalog Card No. 72-95962

International Standard Book Number: 0-87793-051-1

The text of The New American Bible, copyright © 1970 by the Confraternity of Christian Doctrine, Washington, D.C. (Books 1 Samuel to 2 Mac-
cabees, 1969) is reproduced herein by license of said Confraternity of
Christian Doctrine. All rights reserved.

New English translation of the Order of Mass and English translation of
the responsorial antiphons between the readings, the alleluia verses, the
titles, and the summaries of the readings from the Lectionary, copyright
© 1969, International Committee on English in the Liturgy, Inc. All rights
reserved.

Photography: Cover, 10/11, 22, 26, 32, 49, 66, 74, 78, 82, 91, 98, 108
             Anthony Rowland
             2/3 Alpha Corporation
             4/5, 12, 28, 50/51 Joseph R. Fuzey
             16 Terry Barrett
             36, 52, 70, 106, 112/113, 139 Eugene S. Geissler
             38, 56, 94, 114, 132 Mary Ellen Kronstein
             41 Marne Breckensiek
             43, 102, 122 RNS
             62 John Lanzone; 63 Theo Robert; 88/89 Vern Sigl
             92/93 Rose Farkas; 126 Connors; 130 William Conyers.
             136 Rohn Engh

Printed in the United States of America

Contents

RITE OF MASS

Come Celebrate Christ!   10

I. INTRODUCTORY RITES

1. Entrance and Greeting   14
2. Penitential Rite and Forgiveness   18
3. Glory to God and Praise   22

II. LITURGY OF THE WORD

4. Proclaiming the Word of God   28
5. The Homily and the Word   32
6. The Profession of Faith   38
7. General Intercessions   44

III. LITURGY OF THE EUCHARIST

PREPARATION OF THE GIFTS

8. The Gifts of Bread and Wine   52
9. Offering of the Gifts   56
10. Your Sacrifice and Mine   66

THE EUCHARISTIC PRAYER

11. Preface of Praise   74
12. Thanks for God's Mighty Deeds   78
13. Consecration of Bread and Wine   82
14. The People's Proclamation   88
15. The Memorial Prayer   94
16. Prayer for the Living and the Dead   98
17. Doxology and the Great Amen   102

IV. RITE OF COMMUNION

18. The Our Father   108
19. The Sign of Peace   114
20. The Lamb of God   118
21. Invitation to Supper   122
22. The Meal Together   126

V. CONCLUDING RITE

23. The Blessing   132
24. Go . . .   136

LITURGY OF THE WORD . . .

Life of Christ	Liturgical Year

1.	Expecting the Good News	Advent 4 16
2.	Birth of Jesus	Christmas 20
3.	The Baptism of Jesus	Sunday after Epiphany 24
4.	Temptation of Jesus	Lent 1 30
5.	Living Water	Lent 3 34
6.	Sight for the Blind Man	Lent 4 40
7.	Life for Lazarus	Lent 5 46
8.	The Lord's Supper	Holy Thursday 54
9.	Passion and Death of Jesus	Good Friday 58
10.	The Resurrection of the Lord	Easter Vigil 68
11.	Christ Is Alive	Easter Sunday 76
12.	Christ Appears to the Apostles	Easter 2 80
13.	Christ Appears to Two Disciples	Easter 3A 84
14.	Christ Appears the Third Time	Easter 3C 90
15.	Jesus Leaves	Ascension 96
16.	Awaiting the Spirit	Vigil of Pentecost 100
17.	The Spirit Comes	Pentecost Sunday 104
18.	This Is My Body	Corpus Christi 110
19.	Where Shall We Buy Bread . . .?	Season of the Year 17 116
20.	Give Us This Bread Always	Season of the Year 18 120
21.	I Am the Living Bread	Season of the Year 19 124
22.	My Flesh Is Real Food	Season of the Year 20 128
23.	The Multitude of the Blessed	All Saints 134
24.	The Second Coming	Christ the King 138

Together at Mass

No matter what else changes in the Church, the Eucharist remains central. The Mass—as theological reality, as basic act of worship, as primary expression of Christian community—is here to stay.

For generations the piety of Catholics was nourished by this outstanding weekly, if not daily, event and celebration. The missals which Catholics carried back and forth to Mass and often used at home were a mark of the time, as well as a continual source of education and inspiration.

Today the missals are gone, though the need for inspiration and education remains. Yet, for many years now, very little has been written about the Mass for the people.

True, the use of English and other liturgical changes have enabled the people to "hear" the prayers of the Mass and "listen" to the proclamation of the Word of God directly from the altar rather than through the intermediary of a missal. This has been good. The direct relationship between celebrant and people has helped to mold the people of God more closely together in celebration. Yet, the closer working together calls for more and more understanding of what really goes on at Mass.

Together at Mass was put together with two reasons in mind: to fill the vacuum in recent popular literature on the Mass which stood still while the Mass went forward; and to search out the meaning of the Mass and to offer insights into its various parts for a better understanding of this unique Christian assembly—an assembly brought together and made one by the body and the blood and the heartbeat of Jesus, by the Spirit of Christ active among his people.

In this book the Mass is viewed as one thing and as many things. The diversity of answers to such questions as: Why the Mass? What is it? What is its meaning? What does it do? Why is it unique? —reflect both the richness of the Mass and the insights growing out of recent efforts at renewal. Among other perspectives the Mass is viewed as:

—The Christian community assembled around the Word.
—Christ present in the midst of his people.
—God's people gathered together for celebration.
—The central act of the world's worship.
—Prayer of praise and thanks to the Lord.
—Memorial meal and sacrifice.

Against this background the authors comment briefly on a different aspect of each part of the Mass. This makes a total of 48 short columns on the right hand of the page, opposite the rite of the Mass on the left.

The Word of God

After each part of the rite and comments, there follows a selected Liturgy of the Word for the reader's consideration, prayer, and meditation. There are reasons for this.

In her liturgy, the Church rightly puts before us the mystery of Jesus' birth, life, death, rising up to glory, and sending of his Spirit "to recall to our minds everything he said and did." She has, in her wisdom, arranged God's word for our reading and listening in the Mass so that throughout the year the image of Jesus Christ our Lord and Savior would be etched ever more deeply into our consciousness.

The 24 Liturgies of the Word in this book have been carefully chosen according to three principles: 1) They reveal Jesus Christ, 2) they follow the liturgical year, and 3) they reflect the Mass. That all this could be done side by side and in order is itself an indication of the unity that exists between the Mass and Jesus Christ, between the liturgical life of the Church and the events of the life of Christ which the Mass sums up and makes present and active. He who means so much to us and without whom there would be no Mass at all is being continually revealed and made present to us in the faithful worship of the people of God.

It is urged that these Liturgies of the Word be read and listened to with a new attention, one each with the 24 sections of this book on the Mass, as integral to a better understanding of the Mass. We must allow the Word of God to do his work in us. Though an individual Liturgy of the Word will not always "line up exactly" with the particular part of the Mass it stands numerically opposite, it will nevertheless make its contribution to the whole in putting before us Jesus Christ.

Jesus and the Mass

The overall, side-by-side arrangement of the Mass, the life of Christ, and the liturgical year in this book, is as follows:

Introductory Rites: expecting the good news, birth and baptism of Jesus: Advent, Christmas and Epiphany

Liturgy of the Word: public life of Christ: Lent

Preparation of the Gifts: passion-death-resurrection: Holy Week

Eucharistic Prayer: risen life and coming of the Spirit: Easter and Pentecost

Rite of Communion: life in the Spirit: Season of the Year

Concluding Rite: the saints and the second coming: end of the Year.

Photos throughout the book reflect the tensions and themes, the challenges and hopes of living the Mass in today's world, of working for the kingdom of God here and now, while expecting its completion only in a world yet to come.

Come Celebrate Christ!

When the apostles gathered with Jesus in the upper room to celebrate the Passover, there was no doubt in their minds as to what they were about. They met as friends, in the warm and intimate setting of a meal, with one who loved them.

There was ritual, indeed, and some realization that this was no ordinary meal, but what would remain with them long after their hunger was satisfied and the ritual performed was the reality of what Jesus said and did, and the sense of a new relationship with him and with one another. They had experienced Eucharist.

It is often not so with Catholics attending Mass today. True, they know from childhood that the Mass is the central act of Christian life. They know all the doctrinal expressions in which the act of worship is cast: service of the word, offering, sacrifice, communion. But many, if we are to judge by appearance and by their own admission, fail to experience on a personal level what the Mass should be. They do not experience themselves as a worshiping community, a gathering in Christ. They are not conscious of Christ's loving sacrifice being renewed in their midst.

Perhaps with all the attempts at a technical explanation, the most fundamental question has never been adequately or convincingly answered for them: Why do Christians gather for worship? Why the Mass? The answer involves more than official explanations and orthodox terminology, however important. It demands an approach that is sensitive to the deep needs of man—needs which can be filled only by the Spirit of God.

There is no Mass, much less a "celebration" of Mass, without Jesus Christ. It is he who gathers us together; it is he who binds us into one; it is he who is both present and made present again; it is he who moves among us and gives meaning not only to our individual lives, but also to the coming together of his people; it is he who is our past, present, and future because he is yesterday, today, and forever.

In a very real sense, the Church celebrates the whole life-and-death mystery of Christ every time she assembles for Mass. Jesus joined the human race and lives our human life. He is the ever-revealing Word of God. He is the only one who has gone before us through suffering and death to be raised up. He is the one seated at the right hand of the Father who intercedes for us. It is he who sends his Spirit upon us.

The spirit of Jesus is alive and active in the Liturgy of the Word as well as in the Liturgy of the Eucharist. Both are creative in building up the people of God. We must learn once again really to listen to the Word of God because it is a living Word different from all other words. "In the beginning was the Word, and the Word was with God, and the Word was God." Jesus Christ, we know, is the Word made flesh.

It is true, the Word made flesh is not the same as the "words of God" in the bible. Nevertheless, the two are closely related: Through the words of the bible we meet Jesus Christ, the one Word God has spoken. He is the living Word who does his work in us as we listen.

PART 1

Introductory Rites

1. Entrance and Greeting

Entrance song

Then the priest begins:

Priest: In the name of the Father, and of the Son, and of the Holy Spirit.

People: Amen.

Priest: The grace of our Lord Jesus Christ and the love of God and the fellowship of the Holy Spirit be with you all.

People: And also with you.

or

Priest: The grace and peace of God our Father and the Lord Jesus Christ be with you.

People: Blessed be God, the Father of our Lord Jesus Christ.

or

And also with you.

or

Priest: The Lord be with you.

People: And also with you.

GREETING

Why have we come together? Surely one reason is that we need one another. But, most of all, we need Christ. If living has taught us anything, it is that acceptance, forgiveness, love, joy, do not come except through people who have been graced with God's love in Jesus Christ.

But why gather for Mass, for worship? Do not the family dinner, the get-together with friends, the sharing of our everyday lives, each in its own way, serve the need of our being with and sharing love with others, at least some others?

But where is the gathering that satisfies the deepest and most universal need in the hearts of all men to be accepted (and to accept), to be forgiven (and to forgive), to be loved (and to love)—to be one, and to celebrate that oneness? Where is the ultimate gathering where men can offer that perfect sacrifice to God?

The Mass, our faith tells us, is that ultimate gathering, that perfect sacrifice. In the Mass is Christ, the touchstone, the foundation of all wholeness—human and divine. His word, his offering, his power, his redeeming, cross-bearing-unto-death love are there in a special way, under effective signs of reconciliation.

In our time when brother is separated from brother, not only by physical miles but spiritual light-years, we need a gathering where all can come together in peace and love (in yearning, if not yet in fact).

So we gather at Mass, from all over the neighborhood (and from the ends of the earth).

But we do not come together without greeting one another, or we should not. (How can we love another if we do not recognize him?) One way to greet another is with a smile, or a nod. We join in the entrance song with full voice and earnest joy, opening ourselves and making ourselves vulnerable (especially should our song be less than perfect). Our senses, our very humanness, express the desire of our spirit to offer all that we are, all that we have, and all that we can be in union with Christ and our fellowmen.

CALL TO WORSHIP

Man has need to worship. He is a religious being. It is essential that he worship God rather than something less.

Man has need to worship together with others. He is a social being. So he comes together in church, a sacred place, made sacred above all by men coming together for worship.

From among the people a man has been set aside and ordained to lead men in worship. He joins them and greets them, happy to be with them, happy that they have come.

His greeting is a call to worship. Well might he say: "Come, let us worship the Lord; for he is our God and we are his people."

We are all his people, those who have come and those who haven't. Those who have come worship *for* those who haven't. It will always be that way because we represent one another before the Lord.

And when we do . . . we are the salt of the earth! We are the light of the world! We are a royal priesthood!

15

1. Expecting the Good News

(From the Liturgy of the Word for the FOURTH SUNDAY OF ADVENT) **A**

READING I   Is 7:10-14

A reading from the book of the prophet Isaiah
The virgin shall conceive.

The Lord spoke to Ahaz: Ask for a sign from the Lord, your God; let it be deep as the nether world, or high as the sky! But Ahaz answered, "I will not ask! I will not tempt the Lord!" Then he said: Listen, O house of David! Is it not enough for you to weary men, must you also weary my God? Therefore the Lord himself will give you this sign: the virgin shall be with child, and bear a son, and shall name him Immanuel.

This is the Word of the Lord.

Responsorial Psalm   Ps 24:1-2, 3-4, 5-6

R.   *(7:10) Let the Lord enter; he is king of glory.*

The Lord's are the earth and its fullness;
   the world and those who dwell in it.
For he founded it upon the seas
   and established it upon the rivers.

R.   *Let the Lord enter; he is king of glory.*

Who can ascend the mountain of the Lord?
   or who may stand in his holy place?
He whose hands are sinless, whose heart is clean,
   who desires not what is vain.

R.   *Let the Lord enter; he is king of glory.*

He shall receive a blessing from the Lord,
   a reward from God his savior.
Such is the race that seeks for him,
   that seeks the face of the God of Jacob.

R.   *Let the Lord enter; he is king of glory.*

READING II   Rom 1:1-7

The beginning of the letter of Paul to the Romans
Jesus Christ, a descendant of David, is the Son of God.

Greetings from Paul, a servant of Christ Jesus, called to be an apostle and set apart to proclaim the gospel of God which he promised long ago through his prophets, as the holy Scriptures record—the gospel concerning his Son, who was descended from David according to the flesh but was made Son of God in power, according to the spirit of holiness, by his resurrection from the dead: Jesus Christ our Lord. Through him we have been favored with apostleship, that we may spread his name and bring to obedient faith all the Gentiles, among whom are you who have been called to belong to Jesus Christ.

To all in Rome, beloved of God and called to holiness, grace and peace from God our Father and the Lord Jesus Christ.

This is the Word of the Lord.

GOSPEL A   Mt 1:18-24

Alleluia   Mt 1:23

R.   *Alleluia.* A virgin will give birth to a son;
            his name will be Emmanuel: God is
            with us.
R.   *Alleluia.*

✝ *A reading from the holy gospel according to Matthew*

Jesus was born of Mary who was betrothed to Joseph,
a relative of David.

This is how the birth of Jesus Christ came about. When his mother Mary was engaged to Joseph, but before they lived together, she was found with child through the power of the Holy Spirit. Joseph her husband, an upright man unwilling to expose her to the law, decided to divorce her quietly. Such was his intention when suddenly the angel of the Lord appeared in a dream and said to him: "Joseph, son of David, have no fear about taking Mary as your wife. It is by the Holy Spirit that she has conceived this child. She is to have a son and you are to name him Jesus because he will save his people from their sins." All this happened to fulfill what the Lord had said through the prophet:

"The virgin shall be with child
and give birth to a son,
and they shall call him Emmanuel,"

a name which means "God is with us." When Joseph awoke he did as the angel of the Lord had directed him and received her into his home as his wife.

GOSPEL B   Lk 1:26-38

✠ *A reading from the holy gospel according to Luke*
You shall conceive and bear a son.

The angel Gabriel was sent from God to a town of Galilee named Nazareth, to a virgin betrothed to a man named Joseph, of the house of David. The virgin's name was Mary. Upon arriving, the angel said to her: "Rejoice, O highly favored daughter! The Lord is with you. Blessed are you among women." She was deeply troubled by his words, and wondered what his greeting meant. The angel went on to say to her: "Do not fear, Mary. You have found favor with God. You shall conceive and bear a son and give him the name Jesus. Great will be his dignity and he will be called Son of the Most High. The Lord God will give him the throne of David his father. He will rule over the house of Jacob forever and his reign will be without end."

Mary said to the angel, "How can this be since I do not know man?" The angel answered her: "The Holy Spirit will come upon you and the power of the Most High will overshadow you; hence, the holy offspring to be born will be called Son of God. Know that Elizabeth your kins-woman has conceived a son in her old age; she who was thought to be sterile is now in her sixth month, for nothing is impossible with God."

Mary said: "I am the maidservant of the Lord. Let it be done to me as you say." With that the angel left her.

GOSPEL C   Lk 1:39-45

Why should it happen that I am honored with a visit from the mother of my Lord?

Mary set out, proceeding in haste into the hill country to a town of Judah, where she entered Zechariah's house and greeted Elizabeth. When Elizabeth heard Mary's greeting, the baby stirred in her womb. Elizabeth was filled with the Holy Spirit, and cried out in a loud voice: "Blessed are you among women and blessed is the fruit of your womb. But who am I that the mother of my Lord should come to me? The moment your greeting sounded in my ears, the baby stirred in my womb for joy. Blessed is she who trusted that the Lord's words to her would be fulfilled."

This is the gospel of the Lord.

2. Penitential Rite and Forgiveness

Penitential Rite

Priest: My brothers and sisters, to prepare ourselves to celebrate the sacred mysteries, let us call to mind our sins:

After a brief silence, all say:

All: I confess to almighty God,
and to you, my brothers and sisters,
that I have sinned through my own fault
in my thoughts and in my words,
in what I have done,
and in what I have failed to do;
and I ask blessed Mary, ever virgin,
all the angels and saints,
and you, my brothers and sisters,
to pray for me to the Lord our God.

Priest: May almighty God have mercy on us,
forgive us our sins,
and bring us to everlasting life.

People: Amen.

*Other forms of the penitential rite
for optional use:*

Priest: My brothers and sisters, to prepare ourselves to celebrate the sacred mysteries, let us call to mind our sins.

After a brief silence:

Priest: Lord, we have sinned against you:
Lord, have mercy.
People: Lord, have mercy.

Priest: Lord, show us your mercy and love.
People: And grant us your salvation.

Priest: May almighty God have mercy on us,
forgive us our sins,
and bring us to everlasting life.
People: Amen.

or

Priest: My brothers and sisters, to prepare ourselves to celebrate the sacred mysteries, let us call to mind our sins:

After a brief silence:

Priest: You were sent to heal the contrite of heart:
Lord, have mercy.
People: Lord, have mercy.

Priest: You came to call sinners:
Christ, have mercy.
People: Christ, have mercy.

Priest: You plead for us at the right hand of the Father:
Lord, have mercy.
People: Lord, have mercy.

Priest: May almighty God have mercy on us,
forgive us our sins,
and bring us to everlasting life.
People: Amen.

These invocations follow unless they have been used in one of the forms of the act of penance.

Priest: Lord, have mercy.
People: Lord, have mercy.

Priest: Christ, have mercy.
People: Christ, have mercy.

Priest: Lord, have mercy.
People: Lord, have mercy.

RECALLING OUR SINFULNESS

Man has a passion to be "saved," to know that in spite of his sometimes twisted and unruly life, he is accepted and forgiven. Yet we are reluctant to talk about "sin" today.

St. James asserts that there is no truth (and no peace) in the one who says he is without sin. The evidence is all around us: the unkind remark that cuts, the flush that comes when we push anger too far, the prejudice that reddens our faces . . . our damaged pride, the urge to strike back, our self-righteous stand. How often do we feel the disorder of sin in our very bones? How often must we say with the apostle Paul: "The evil that I would not, that I do"?

That evil extends much farther than our individual persons into family strife, civic disorder, racism, war . . .

There is a remedy for this cancerous running on. God loved us "even when we were in sin," and he has accepted and forgiven us, especially in Jesus. "Here is a saying," Paul assures us, "that you can rely on and nobody should doubt: Christ Jesus came into the world to save sinners." We are here precisely to acknowledge this tremendous goodness of our God, to celebrate it, to make ourselves ever more aware of it in order to participate in it more fully. But we ought first to admit our sin.

The gospel suggests that if we have anything against our brother we ought first to go and reconcile ourselves with him, and then come and offer our gift. At least let us recall our faults, repent of them, and renew our resolve to love our "brother": our spouse, our children, the neighbor next door, our fellow worker, our relatives and friends, the poor, the unwanted, the downtrodden of this world.

Then let us ask for mercy.

CONFESSION AND FORGIVENESS

"As long as nobody gets hurt . . ." the young generation sometimes says.

But someone always gets hurt. We are limited. What we do for one, we deny another because there isn't enough of us to go around.

Maybe we don't hurt the person before us, but by the same action we hurt someone not present.

Or we think we don't hurt the one present and immediately involved with us, only to discover later that our action more remotely had some bad results—and injured him.

"Forgive us as we forgive each other," the Lord has taught us. We are all sinners. We sin all the time. Somebody is always getting hurt in some way.

"I confess to . . . God, and to you my brothers. . . ." To confess to God is already to be forgiven by God (who never ceased to love us).

To confess to my brothers is to ask forgiveness and perhaps to have to wait to be forgiven. A brother's hurts are not always healed that easily.

We pray together to be healed and reconciled.

19

2. Birth of Jesus

(From the Liturgy of the Word for CHRISTMAS AT MIDNIGHT) **A B C**

READING I   Is 9:1-6

A reading from the book of the prophet Isaiah
A son is given to us.

The people who walked in darkness
   have seen a great light;
Upon those who dwelt in the land of gloom
   a light has shone.
You have brought them abundant joy
   and great rejoicing,
As they rejoice before you as at the harvest,
   as men make merry when dividing spoils.
For the yoke that burdened them,
   the pole on their shoulder,
And the rod of their taskmaster
   you have smashed, as on the day of Midian.
For every boot that tramped in battle,
   every cloak rolled in blood,
      will be burned as fuel for flames.

For a child is born to us, a son is given us;
   upon his shoulder dominion rests.
They name him Wonder-Counselor, God-Hero,
   Father-Forever, Prince of Peace.
His dominion is vast
   and forever peaceful,
From David's throne, and over his kingdom,
   which he confirms and sustains
By judgment and justice,
   both now and forever.
The zeal of the Lord of hosts will do this!

This is the Word of the Lord.

Responsorial Psalm   Ps 96:1-2, 2-3, 11-12, 13

R. *(Luke 2:11) Today is born our Savior, Christ the Lord.*

Sing to the Lord a new song;
   sing to the Lord, all you lands.
Sing to the Lord; bless his name.

R. *Today is born our Savior, Christ the Lord.*

Announce his salvation, day after day.
   Tell his glory among the nations;
Among all peoples, his wondrous deeds.

R. *Today is born our Savior, Christ the Lord.*

Let the heavens be glad and the earth rejoice;
   let the sea and what fills it resound;
   let the plains be joyful and all that is in them!
Then shall all the trees of the forest exult.

R. *Today is born our Savior, Christ the Lord.*

They shall exult before the Lord, for he comes;
   for he comes to rule the earth.
He shall rule the world with justice
   and the peoples with his constancy.

R. *Today is born our Savior, Christ the Lord.*

READING II   Ti 2:11-14

A reading from the letter of Paul to Titus
God's grace has been revealed to all men.

The grace of God has appeared, offering salvation to all men. It trains us to reject godless ways and worldly desires, and live temperately, justly, and devoutly in this age as we await our blessed hope, the appearing of the glory of the great God and of our Savior Christ Jesus. It was he who sacrificed himself for us, to redeem us from all unrighteousness and to cleanse for himself a people of his own, eager to do what is right.

This is the Word of the Lord.

GOSPEL (Mass at Midnight)   **Lk 2:1-14**

Alleluia   Lk 2:10-11

R.   *Alleluia.* Good News and great joy to all the
world:
today is born our Savior, Christ the Lord.
R.   *Alleluia.*

✠ *A reading from the holy gospel according to
Luke*
Today a savior has been born for you.

In those days Caesar Augustus published a decree
ordering a census of the whole world. This first
census took place while Quirinius was governor
of Syria. Everyone went to register, each to his
own town. And so Joseph went from the town of
Nazareth in Galilee to Judea, to David's town of
Bethlehem—because he was of the house and
lineage of David—to register with Mary, his
espoused wife, who was with child.

While they were there the days of her confine-
ment were completed. She gave birth to her firstborn son and wrapped him in swaddling clothes
and laid him in a manger, because there was no
room for them in the place where travelers lodged.

There were shepherds in the locality, living in
the fields and keeping night watch by turns over
their flock. The angel of the Lord appeared to
them, as the glory of the Lord shone around
them, and they were very much afraid. The angel
said to them: "You have nothing to fear! I come
to proclaim good news to you—tidings of great
joy to be shared by the whole people. This day
in David's city a savior has been born to you,
the Messiah and Lord. Let this be a sign to you:
in a manger you will find an infant wrapped in
swaddling clothes." Suddenly, there was with the
angel a multitude of the heavenly host, praising
God and saying,
"Glory to God in high heaven,
peace on earth to those on whom his favor
rests."

GOSPEL (Mass at Dawn)   **Lk 2:15-28**

The shepherds found Mary and Joseph, and the baby,
lying in the manger.

When the angels had returned to heaven, the
shepherds said to one another: "Let us go over to
Bethlehem and see this event which the Lord has
made known to us." They went in haste and
found Mary and Joseph, and the baby lying in the
manger; once they saw, they understood what had
been told them concerning this child. All who
heard of it were astonished at the report given
them by the shepherds.

Mary treasured all these things and reflected
on them in her heart. The shepherds returned,
glorifying and praising God for all they had
heard and seen, in accord with what had been
told them.

This is the gospel of the Lord.

21

3. Glory to God and Praise

Then, when it is prescribed:

Glory to God in the highest,
    and peace to his people on earth.
Lord God, heavenly King,
almighty God and Father,
    we worship you, we give you thanks,
    we praise you for your glory.
Lord Jesus Christ, only Son of the Father,
Lord God, Lamb of God,
you take away the sin of the world:
    have mercy on us;
you are seated at the right hand of the Father:
    receive our prayer.
For you alone are the Holy One,
you alone are the Lord,
you alone are the Most High,
    Jesus Christ,
    with the Holy Spirit,
    in the glory of God the Father.
    Amen.

WE PRAISE GOD

We praise God, we thank him. Certainly not for any need that he might have, but for the need we have.

A glowing sunset, the majesty of a mountain, the touch of an infant's hand move even the densest of men. There is such beauty and goodness in the world that God created, both in nature and in grace, that reflection on it practically forces a response. If we are silent, "the very stones will cry out!"

Therefore, here at the beginning of Mass, we appropriately praise and thank God and call down peace upon his people.

We praise the Father for his creation and for having revealed to us his love and mercy.

We thank the Son for taking away our sins.

We court the Spirit for his continuing presence among us.

We expect great things to come.

We look on our fellowmen and remind ourselves, as the folk song has it, "Everyone's beautiful in their own particular way," because every person is a reflection of God.

Look around you and find many reasons to praise and thank him.

THE GOODNESS OF GOD

Because God has first loved us, we are, and he loves us once for all. Whether we love him or not, he loves us. His name is love.

But we *do* love him, for to know him is to love him. Whatever we know of friendship and goodness . . . whatever we know of joy and peace and beauty—has put us in touch with God.

If we delight in wind, sun, rain, the ocean . . . if we delight in the human body . . . if we cherish ourselves, thrill with our beloved, play with our children—we are praising God.

If we are celebrating at a party, he is there. Because his delight is to be with the children of men, there is no celebration without him.

Where love is, there is God. We have come together to celebrate truth, beauty, goodness, in all their forms and in their ultimate form in the world.

With a hymn of praise directed for the most part to the Lord Jesus Christ, we recognize God's intimate presence in each of us, and in all of us together. But most of all we acknowledge God's greatness, glory and mercy.

3. The Baptism of Jesus

(From the Liturgy of the Word for the SUNDAY AFTER EPIPHANY) **A B C**

READING I   Is 42:1-4, 6-7

A reading from the book of the prophet Isaiah
Here is my servant, my chosen one in whom
my soul delights.

Here is my servant whom I uphold,
    my chosen one with whom I am pleased,
Upon whom I have put my spirit;
    he shall bring forth justice to the nations,
Not crying out, not shouting,
    not making his voice heard in the street.
A bruised reed he shall not break,
    and a smoldering wick he shall not quench,
Until he establishes justice on the earth;
    the coastlands will wait for his teaching.

I, the Lord, have called you for the victory of
    justice,
    I have grasped you by the hand;
I formed you, and set you
    as a covenant of the people,
    a light for the nations,
To open the eyes of the blind,
    to bring out prisoners from confinement,
    and from the dungeon, those who live in
        darkness.

This is the Word of the Lord.

Responsorial Psalm   Ps 29:1-2, 3-4, 3, 9-10

R. *(11) The Lord will bless his people with
    peace.*

Give to the Lord, you sons of God,
    give to the Lord glory and praise,
Give to the Lord the glory due his name;
    adore the Lord in holy attire.

R. *The Lord will bless his people with peace.*

The voice of the Lord is over the waters,
    the Lord, over vast waters.
The voice of the Lord is mighty;
    the voice of the Lord is majestic.

R. *The Lord will bless his people with peace.*

The God of glory thunders,
    and in his temple all say, "Glory!"
The Lord is enthroned above the flood;
    the Lord is enthroned as king forever.

R. *The Lord will bless his people with peace.*

READING II   Acts 10:34-38

A reading from the Acts of the Apostles
God anointed him with the Holy Spirit and with power.

Peter addressed Cornelius and the people assembled at his house in these words: "I begin to see how true it is that God shows no partiality. Rather, the man of any nation who fears God and acts uprightly is acceptable to him. This is the message he has sent to the sons of Israel, 'the good news of peace' proclaimed through Jesus Christ who is Lord of all. I take it you know what has been reported all over Judea about Jesus of Nazareth, beginning in Galilee with the baptism John preached; of the way God anointed him with the Holy Spirit and power. He went about doing good works and healing all who were in the grip of the devil, and God was with him.

This is the Word of the Lord.

GOSPEL A   Mt 3:13-17

Alleluia   See Mk 9:6

R.   *Alleluia.* The heavens were opened and the
        Father's voice was heard:
        this is my beloved Son, hear him.
R.   *Alleluia.*

✠ *A reading from the holy gospel according to
Matthew*

When Jesus was baptized the heavens were opened and
the Spirit of God came upon him.

Jesus, coming from Galilee, appeared before John
at the Jordan to be baptized by him. John tried
to refuse him with the protest, "I should be baptized by you, yet you come to me!" Jesus answered, "Give in for now. We must do this if we
would fulfill all of God's demands." So John gave
in. After Jesus was baptized, he came directly
out of the water. Suddenly the sky opened and he
saw the Spirit of God descend like a dove and
hover over him. With that, a voice from the
heavens said, "This is my beloved Son. My favor
rests on him."

GOSPEL B   Mk 1:7-11

✠ *A reading from the holy gospel according to
Mark*

You are my Son, the beloved; my favor rests on you.

The theme of John's preaching was: "One more
powerful than I is to come after me. I am not fit
to stoop and untie his sandal straps. I have baptized you in water; he will baptize you in the Holy
Spirit."

During that time, Jesus came from Nazareth
in Galilee and was baptized in the Jordan by
John. Immediately on coming up out of the water
he saw the sky rent in two and the Spirit descend-
ing on him like a dove. Then a voice came from
the heavens: "You are my beloved Son. On you
my favor rests."

GOSPEL C   Lk 3:15-16, 21-22

✠ *A reading from the holy gospel according to
Luke*

Someone is coming who is more powerful than I am, he will
baptize you with the Holy Spirit and with fire.

The people were full of anticipation, wondering
in their hearts whether John might be the Messiah. John answered them all by saying: "I am
baptizing you in water, but there is one to come
who is mightier than I. I am not fit to loosen his
sandal strap. He will baptize you in the Holy
Spirit and in fire."

When all the people were baptized, and Jesus
was at prayer after likewise being baptized, the
skies opened and the Holy Spirit descended on
him in visible form like a dove. A voice from
heaven was heard to say, "You are my beloved
Son. On you my favor rests."

This is the gospel of the Lord.

Filled with the Holy Spirit

PART 2

Liturgy of the Word

4. Proclaiming the Word of God

LITURGY OF THE WORD

To indicate the end of the reading, the reader says:

Reader: This is the Word of the Lord.
All: Thanks be to God.

The psalm is then sung or recited. If there is a second reading, the reader adds:

Reader: This is the Word of the Lord.
All: Thanks be to God.

The alleluia or other chant follows. The Gospel is then read:

Priest: The Lord be with you.
People: And also with you.

Priest: A reading from the holy gospel according to N.
People: Glory to you, Lord.

At the end of the Gospel:

Priest: This is the Gospel of the Lord.
People: Praise to you, Lord Jesus Christ.

THE READINGS

From the time when man walked and talked with God in the garden, he has treasured God's presence. Man, the pilgrim, falters without a secure hold, without direction.

Our Jewish ancestors, the people of God of old, had the Ark of the Covenant and the tables of the law which they carried to remind them that their God, their rock, defender and guide, was near.

We have the Scriptures and the Eucharist. Our God is near, especially at Mass.

But the Scriptures (and what we do at Mass) are more complex than at first we understood. God speaks to us . . . but the sacred writings contain more than the words which are preceded by "God said."

The Scriptures are a record of what God *did,* of what God did among men, and of what he is *doing* among men. They are a record of his life among men. God has spoken not only in words, but in people, in events, in the saving history in which we are all involved. We ought to experience this at Mass.

One of the great anxieties of our time is man's feeling of rootlessness. No one cares, he thinks in times of despair, not even God . . . if, indeed, God is not dead. Man may have a home, a place to be himself, a family in which to find himself, and friends . . . yet the feeling persists.

The reason for our restlessness is that we have roots deeper than our immediate forebears. We have been around longer than our age would imply and will remain beyond our fleeting years. We have a past and a future, a family history, a link with all humanity, past, present and future, at least in hope.

Moses, Isaiah, Matthew, Mark, Luke, John, Peter, Paul tell us of that family history. "At various times in the past and in various different ways, God spoke to our ancestors through the prophets; but in our own time, the last days, he has spoken to us through his Son."

THE BIBLE

The bible is the perennial best seller of all time. Why?

Good literature? Famous author(s)? Good story? Wide range of human interest? Popular appeal? Significant social contribution? Yes, yes, yes.

Full of meaning? Historically important? An exciting achievement? Landmark? Prize winner? Milestone? Yes, yes, yes.

But why really?

It is "God's book," the word of God, the revelation of God to man.

From it we learn of our beginnings, we learn of the God who first loved us. We learn of Jesus, the Son of God. In it we find an explanation of man, the meaning of man.

The bible is our story, our family history. It shows forth the humanity of God in his dealings and relationships with man, his interventions in history.

He is our God and we are his people. His word is power and light and sweetness.

4. Temptation of Jesus

*(From the Liturgy of the Word for the
FIRST SUNDAY OF LENT)*   **A**

READING I   Gn 2:7-9; 3:1-7

A reading from the book of Genesis
Creation of our first parents, and Sin.

The Lord God formed man out of the clay of the ground and blew into his nostrils the breath of life, and so man became a living being.

Then the Lord God planted a garden in Eden, in the east, and he placed there the man whom he had formed. Out of the ground the Lord God made various trees grow that were delightful to look at and good for food, with the tree of life in the middle of the garden and the tree of the knowledge of good and bad.

Now the serpent was the most cunning of all the animals that the Lord God had made. The serpent asked the woman, "Did God really tell you not to eat from any of the trees in the garden?" The woman answered the serpent: "We may eat of the fruit of the trees in the garden; it is only about the fruit of the tree in the middle of the garden that God said, 'You shall not eat it or even touch it, lest you die.'" But the serpent said to the woman: "You certainly will not die! No, God knows well that the moment you eat of it you will be like gods who know what is good and what is bad." The woman saw that the tree was good for food, pleasing to the eyes, and desirable for gaining wisdom. So she took some of its fruit and ate it; and she also gave some to her husband, who was with her, and he ate it. Then the eyes of both of them were opened, and they realized that they were naked; so they sewed fig leaves together and made loincloths for themselves.

This is the Word of the Lord.

Responsorial Psalm   Ps 51:3-4, 5-6, 12-13, 14, 17

R. *(3) Be merciful, O Lord, for we have sinned.*

Have mercy on me, O God, in your goodness;
  in the greatness of your compassion wipe out
    my offense.
Thoroughly wash me from my guilt
  and of my sin cleanse me.

R. *Be merciful, O Lord, for we have sinned.*

For I acknowledge my offense,
  and my sin is before me always:
"Against you only have I sinned,
  and done what is evil in your sight."

R. *Be merciful, O Lord, for we have sinned.*

A clean heart create for me, O God,
  and a steadfast spirit renew within me.
Cast me not out from your presence,
  and your holy spirit take not from me.

R. *Be merciful, O Lord, for we have sinned.*

Give me back the joy of your salvation,
  and a willing spirit sustain in me.
O Lord, open my lips,
  and my mouth shall proclaim your praise.

R. *Be merciful, O Lord, for we have sinned.*

A reading from the letter of Paul to the Romans
The results of the gift, Jesus Christ, outweigh one man's sin.

Through one man sin entered the world and with sin death, death thus coming to all men inasmuch as all sinned—before the law there was sin in the world, even though sin is not imputed when there is no law—I say, from Adam to Moses death reigned, even over those who had not sinned by breaking a precept as did Adam, that type of the Man to come.

But the gift is not like the offense. For if by the offense of the one man all died, much more did the grace of God and the gracious gift of the one man, Jesus Christ, abound for all. The gift is entirely different from the sin committed by the one man. In the first case, sentence followed upon one offense and brought condemnation, but in the second, the gift came after many offenses and brought acquittal. If death began its reign through one man because of his offense, much more shall those who receive the overflowing grace and gift of justice live and reign through the one man, Jesus Christ. To sum up, then: just as a single offense brought condemnation to all men, a single righteous act brought all men acquittal and life. Just as through one man's disobedience all became sinners, so through one man's obedience all shall become just.

This is the Word of the Lord.

Verse before the Gospel   Mt 4:4

Man does not live on bread alone,
but on every word that comes from the mouth of God.

✠ *A reading from the holy gospel according to Matthew*
Jesus fasted for forty days and nights.

Jesus was led into the desert by the Spirit to be tempted by the devil. He fasted forty days and forty nights, and afterward was hungry. The tempter approached and said to him, "If you are the Son of God, command these stones to turn into bread." Jesus replied, "Scripture has it:
   'Not on bread alone is man to live
     but on every utterance that comes from the mouth of God.' "
Next the devil took him to the holy city, set him on the parapet of the temple, and said, "If you are the Son of God, throw yourself down. Scripture has it:
   'He will bid his angels take care of you;
     with their hands they will support you that you may never stumble on a stone.' "
Jesus answered him, "Scripture also has it:
   'You shall not put the Lord your God to the test.' "
The devil then took him to a lofty mountain peak and displayed before him all the kingdoms of the world in their magnificence, promising, "All these will I bestow on you if you prostrate yourself in homage before me." At this, Jesus said to him, "Away with you, Satan! Scripture says:
   'You shall do homage to the Lord your God;
     him alone shall you adore.' "
At that the devil left him, and angels came and waited on him.

This is the gospel of the Lord.

5. The Homily and the Word

A homily shall be given on all Sundays and holy days of obligation; it is recommended for other days.

PREACHING THE WORD

The word is power. There is little doubt about that in a time when a word can cause a revolution. The people will move toward "peace" or "justice for all" or "clean air" when the time is right, when the word expresses an idea whose time has come.

The inspired word of God is power, too. God said, "Let there be light" and light was made. When we hear the word of God something happens in us . . . if our heart is right. And because we hear the word, something will happen in the world too, in God's good time.

The readings at Mass, the Church teaches, are the word of God. They are powerful . . . if we will listen.

But to be heard effectively today, the word of God has to be translated into terms we can understand in our situation. It has to be translated into what God wants to say to us *here and now*. It is God's word, but God speaks in the language of man.

Men sometimes use the word rather than proclaim it. But God's word, like God himself, will not be "used" to push any man's pride, to back any man's prejudice. God's word is a "two-edged sword." It cuts to the heart and to the marrow; it judges all thoughts. Today, more than ever, we need the word that reconciles rather than the rhetoric that separates.

"You have heard it said . . . but I say to you, love your enemies, do good to those who hate you and say all manner of things against you."

How do we know when it is God who speaks?

We can be sure that God is speaking—in anyone's language, and in the humblest attempt to communicate—if the result is an effective call to love, to witness, to openness, to service, to truth, to humility, to understanding, to a passion for justice, to the wisdom of creative suffering . . . to the will to reach ever more deeply into life and people and God so that "all things may be restored in Christ."

LISTENING TO THE WORD

We expect both too much and too little from the priest stepping forward to give the homily.

We expect too much when we expect him to entertain us now with story and rhetoric, to transform himself into something he is not, or to give back to us only our own prejudices in what the scriptural readings mean.

We expect too little when we don't expect him to be prepared. It is his business to know more about the time, place and peculiar circumstances of the original setting of the readings than we do. We expect too little as well when we don't expect him to translate the message into present terms, to clarify concretely the meaning and how it applies to us right now.

Still, for our part, we have to listen, really listen, not just to the priest and his always too meager words, but to the Spirit who is always active wherever the word of God is being spoken and being talked about.

No matter what else may be wrong, the Spirit is present among us gathered together, and he is ready to in-spirit us with the truth of life.

5. Living Water

(From the Liturgy of the Word for the THIRD SUNDAY OF LENT)

A

READING 1   Ex 17:3-7

A reading from the book of Exodus
Give us water to drink.

In their thirst for water, the people grumbled against Moses, saying, "Why did you ever make us leave Egypt? Was it just to have us die here of thirst with our children and our livestock?" So Moses cried out to the Lord, "What shall I do with this people? A little more and they will stone me!" The Lord answered Moses, "Go over there in front of the people, along with some of the elders of Israel, holding in your hand, as you go, the staff with which you struck the river. I will be standing there in front of you on the rock in Horeb. Strike the rock, and the water will flow from it for the people to drink." This Moses did, in the presence of the elders of Israel. The place was called Massah and Meribah, because the Israelites quarreled there and tested the Lord, saying, "Is the Lord in our midst or not?"

This is the Word of the Lord.

Responsorial Psalm   Ps 95:1-2, 6-7, 8-9

R.   *(8) If today you hear his voice, harden not your hearts.*

Come, let us sing joyfully to the Lord;
    let us acclaim the Rock of our salvation.
Let us greet him with thanksgiving;
    let us joyfully sing psalms to him.

R.   *If today you hear his voice, harden not your hearts.*

Come, let us bow down in worship;
    let us kneel before the Lord who made us.
For he is our God,
    and we are the people he shepherds, the flock he guides.

R.   *If today you hear his voice, harden not your hearts.*

Oh, that today you would hear his voice:
    "Harden not your hearts as at Meribah, as in the day of Massah in the desert,
Where your fathers tempted me;
    they tested me though they had seen my works.

R.   *If today you hear his voice, harden not your hearts.*

READING II   **Rom 5:1-2, 5-8**

A reading from the letter of Paul to the Romans
The love of God has been poured into our hearts by the Holy Spirit which has been given to us.

Now that we have been justified by faith, we are at peace with God through our Lord Jesus Christ. Through him we have gained access by faith to the grace in which we now stand, and we boast of our hope for the glory of God. And this hope will not leave us disappointed, because the love of God has been poured out in our hearts through the Holy Spirit who has been given to us. At the appointed time, when we were still powerless, Christ died for us godless men. It is rare that anyone should lay down his life for a just man, though it is barely possible that for a good man someone may have the courage to die. It is precisely in this that God proves his love for us: that while we were still sinners, Christ died for us.

This is the Word of the Lord.

GOSPEL   **Jn 4:5-42**

Verse before the Gospel   *Jn 4:42, 15*

Lord, you are truly the Savior of the world;
give me living water, that I may never thirst again.

✠ *A reading from the holy gospel according to John*
The water that I shall give will turn into a spring of eternal life.

Jesus had to pass through Samaria, and his journey brought him to a Samaritan town named Shechem near the plot of land which Jacob had given to his son Joseph. This was the site of Jacob's well. Jesus, tired from his journey, sat down at the well.

The hour was about noon. When a Samaritan woman came to draw water, Jesus said to her, "Give me a drink." (His disciples had gone off to the town to buy provisions.) The Samaritan woman said to him, "You are a Jew. How can you ask me, a Samaritan and a woman, for a drink?" (Recall that Jews have nothing to do with Samaritans.) Jesus replied:
  "If only you recognized God's gift,
    and who it is that is asking you for a drink,
    you would have asked him instead,
    and he would have given you living water."
"Sir," she challenged him, "you don't have a bucket and this well is deep. Where do you expect to get this flowing water? Surely you don't pretend to be greater than our ancestor Jacob, who gave us this well and drank from it with his sons and his flocks?" Jesus replied:
  "Everyone who drinks this water
    will be thirsty again.
  But whoever drinks the water I give him will
    never be thirsty;

no, the water I give
shall become a fountain within him,
leaping up to provide eternal life."
The woman said to him, "Give me this water, sir, so that I won't grow thirsty and have to keep coming here to draw water."

He told her, "Go, call your husband, and then come back here." "I have no husband," replied the woman. "You are right in saying you have no husband!" Jesus exclaimed. "The fact is, you have had five, and the man you are living with now is not your husband. What you said is true enough."

"Sir," answered the woman, "I can see you are a prophet. Our ancestors worshiped on this mountain, but you people claim that Jerusalem is the place where men ought to worship God." Jesus told her:

"Believe me, woman,
an hour is coming
when you will worship the Father
neither on this mountain
nor in Jerusalem.
You people worship what you do not under-
    stand,
while we understand what we worship;
after all, salvation is from the Jews.
Yet an hour is coming, and is already here,
when authentic worshipers
will worship the Father in Spirit and truth.
Indeed, it is just such worshipers
the Father seeks.
God is Spirit,
and those who worship him
must worship in Spirit and truth."

The woman said to him: "I know there is a Messiah coming. (This term means Anointed.) When he comes, he will tell us everything." Jesus replied, "I who speak to you am he."

His disciples, returning at this point, were surprised that Jesus was speaking with a woman. No one put a question, however, such as "What do you want of him?" or "Why are you talking with her?" The woman then left her water jar and went off into the town. She said to the people: "Come and see someone who told me everything I ever did! Could this not be the Messiah?" With that they set out from the town to meet him.

Meanwhile the disciples were urging him, "Rabbi, eat something." But he told them:
"I have food to eat
of which you do not know."
At this the disciples said to one another, "You do not suppose anyone has brought him something to eat?" Jesus explained to them:
"Doing the will of him who sent me
and bringing his work to completion
is my food.
Do you not have a saying:
'Four months more
and it will be harvest!'?
Listen to what I say:
Open your eyes and see!
The fields are shining for harvest!
The reaper already collects his wages
and gathers a yield for eternal life,
that sower and reaper may rejoice together.
Here we have the saying verified:
'One man sows; another reaps.'
I sent you to reap
what you had not worked for.
Others have done the labor,
and you have come into their gain."
Many Samaritans from that town believed in him on the strength of the woman's word of testimony: "He told me everything I ever did." The result was that, when these Samaritans came to him, they begged him to stay with them awhile. So he stayed there two days, and through his own spoken word many more came to faith. As they told the woman: "No longer does our faith depend on your story. We have heard for ourselves, and we know that this really is the Savior of the world."

This is the gospel of the Lord.

6. The Profession of Faith

After the homily, the profession of faith is made if prescribed:

We believe in one God,
 the Father, the Almighty,
 maker of heaven and earth,
 of all that is seen and unseen.

We believe in one Lord, Jesus Christ,
 the only Son of God,
 eternally begotten of the Father,
 God from God, Light from Light,
 true God from true God,
 begotten, not made, one in Being
  with the Father.
 Through him all things were made.
 For us men and for our salvation
  he came down from heaven:
 by the power of the Holy Spirit
  he was born of the Virgin Mary,
   and became man.
 For our sake he was crucified under
  Pontius Pilate;
 he suffered, died, and was buried.
 On the third day he rose again
  in fulfillment of the Scriptures;
 He ascended into heaven
  and is seated at the right hand
   of the Father.
 He will come again in glory to judge
  the living and the dead,
  and his kingdom will have no end.

We believe in the Holy Spirit, the Lord,
 the giver of life,
 who proceeds from the Father and the Son.
 With the Father and the Son he is worshiped
  and glorified.

 He has spoken through the Prophets.
We believe in one holy catholic and
  apostolic Church.
 We acknowledge one baptism for the
  forgiveness of sins.
 We look for the resurrection of the dead,
  and the life of the world to come. Amen.

SOMEONE TO BELIEVE IN

There was a time when we studied the Creed mostly as a catalogue of "truths" to be believed. Now we understand that it is also the revealing history of Someone to *believe in*.

You can believe the truth that God is Father, but unless you ponder all he has done, you will not begin to experience him as a father deserving your confidence.

Indeed, God created the world, as he ordered all things in it under man's dominion. But what good if man does not at times, at least, consciously touch his ever-active and sustaining presence?

Truthfully, God became one of us and suffered and died "for our sake," but how weak is your faith until you can begin to trace his features in the universe he has made and the people he has loved.

Surely you can believe that the Spirit is here animating this community gathering and confirming us in our love and service of one another. But it takes a complete response of mind and heart.

We have been born into God's family through creation, initiated into this Christian community through baptism, nourished and sustained in the Risen Christ through the ministry of our priests and our ministry to one another. But we will not really experience this holy relationship until we begin to live it in our homes and in our work.

THE CREED

Our creed is a mighty creed about a mighty God.

It is, once you really think about it—incredible. And that is what makes it a profession of faith.

"I believe in one God the Father Almighty (not maker of bridges, or builder of skyscrapers, or stacker of fortunes, or molder of civilizations; not king, dictator, astronaut, but . . .) maker of heaven and earth." Incredible!

"And in Jesus Christ, his only son . . . born of a virgin." Unbelievable! "And on the third day he rose from the dead." Fantastic!

"And in the Holy Spirit, Lord and giver of life."

"And in the resurrection of the dead and life everlasting." Who can believe that?

We not only can, but do believe, because God himself has taught us to reach for the stars—believing the unbelievable, dreaming the impossible, living forever because God is God.

6. Sight for the Blind Man

*(From the Liturgy of the Word for the
FOURTH SUNDAY OF LENT)* **A**

READING I 1 Sm 16:1, 6-7, 10-13

A reading from the first book of Samuel
In the presence of the Lord God, they anointed
David king of Israel.

The Lord said to Samuel: "I am sending you to
Jesse of Bethlehem, for I have chosen my king
from among his sons."

As Jesse and his sons came to the sacrifice,
Samuel looked at Eliab and thought, "Surely the
Lord's anointed is here before him." But the Lord
said to Samuel: "Do not judge from his appearance or from his lofty stature, because I have rejected him. Not as man sees does God see, because man sees the appearance but the Lord looks
into the heart." In the same way Jesse presented
seven sons before Samuel, but Samuel said to
Jesse, "The Lord has not chosen any one of
these." Then Samuel asked Jesse, "Are these all
the sons you have?" Jesse replied, "There is still
the youngest, who is tending the sheep." Samuel
said to Jesse, "Send for him; we will not begin the
sacrificial banquet until he arrives here." Jesse
sent and had the young man brought to them. He
was ruddy, a youth handsome to behold and
making a splendid appearance. The Lord said,
"There—anoint him, for this is he!" Then Samuel, with the horn of oil in hand, anointed him
in the midst of his brothers; and from that day
on, the spirit of the Lord rushed upon David.

This is the Word of the Lord.

Responsorial Psalm Ps 23:1-3, 3-4, 5, 6

R. *(1) The Lord is my shepherd, there is nothing I shall want.*

The Lord is my shepherd; I shall not want.
  In verdant pastures he gives me repose;
Beside restful waters he leads me;
  he refreshes my soul.

R. *The Lord is my shepherd, there is nothing
I shall want.*

He guides me in right paths
  for his name's sake.
Even though I walk in the dark valley
  I fear no evil; for you are at my side
With your rod and your staff
  that give me courage.

R. *The Lord is my shepherd, there is nothing
I shall want.*

You spread the table before me
  in the sight of my foes;
You anoint my head with oil;
  my cup overflows.

R. *The Lord is my shepherd, there is nothing
I shall want.*

Only goodness and kindness follow me
  all the days of my life;
And I shall dwell in the house of the Lord
  for years to come.

R. *The Lord is my shepherd, there is nothing
I shall want.*

READING II   Eph 5:8-14

A reading from the letter of Paul to the Ephesians
Rise from the dead, and Christ will shine on you.

There was a time when you were darkness, but
now you are light in the Lord. Well, then, live as
children of light. Light produces every kind of
goodness and justice and truth. Be correct in your
judgment of what pleases the Lord. Take no part
in vain deeds done in darkness; rather, condemn
them. It is shameful even to mention the things
these people do in secret; but when such deeds
are condemned, they are seen in the light of day,
and all that then appears is light. That is why we
read:

"Awake, O sleeper,
      arise from the dead,
      and Christ will give you light."

This is the Word of the Lord.

GOSPEL   Jn 9:1-41

Verse before the Gospel   Jn 8:12

I am the light of the world, says the Lord:
the man who follows me will have the light of
      life.

✠ *A reading from the holy gospel according to
      John*

The blind man went off and washed himself and came away
with his sight restored.

As Jesus walked along, he saw a man who had
been blind from birth. His disciples asked him,
"Rabbi, was it his sin or his parents' that caused
him to be born blind?" "Neither," answered
Jesus:

41

"It was no sin, either of this man or of his parents.
Rather, it was to let God's works show forth in him.
We must do the deeds of him who sent me while it is day.
The night comes on
when no one can work.
While I am in the world
I am the light of the world."
With that Jesus spat on the ground, made mud with his saliva, and smeared the man's eyes with the mud. Then he told him, "Go, wash in the pool of Siloam." (This name means "One who has been sent.") So the man went off and washed, and came back able to see.

His neighbors and the people who had been accustomed to see him begging began to ask, "Isn't this the fellow who used to sit and beg?" Some were claiming it was he; others maintained it was not but someone who looked like him. The man himself said, "I'm the one, all right." They said to him then, "How were your eyes opened?" He answered: "That man they call Jesus made mud and smeared it on my eyes, telling me to go to Siloam and wash. When I did go and wash, I was able to see." "Where is he?" they asked. He replied, "I have no idea."

Next, they took the man, who had been born blind, to the Pharisees. (Note that it was on a sabbath that Jesus had made the mud paste and opened his eyes.) The Pharisees, in turn, began to inquire how he had recovered his sight. He told them, "He put mud on my eyes. I washed it off, and now I can see." This prompted some of the Pharisees to assert, "This man cannot be from God because he does not keep the sabbath." Others objected, "If a man is a sinner, how can he perform signs like these?" They were sharply divided over him. Then they addressed the blind man again: "Since it was your eyes he opened, what do you have to say about him?" "He is a prophet," he replied.

The Jews refused to believe that he had really been born blind and had begun to see, until they summoned the parents of this man who now could see. "Is this your son?" they asked, "and if so, do you attest that he was blind at birth? How do you account for the fact that he now can see?" His parents answered, "We know this is our son, and we know he was blind at birth. But how he can see now, or who opened his eyes, we have no idea. Ask him. He is old enough to speak for himself." (His parents answered in this fashion because they were afraid of the Jews, who had already agreed among themselves that anyone who acknowledged Jesus as the Messiah would be put out of the synagogue. That was why his parents said, "He is of age—ask him.")

A second time they summoned the man who had been born blind and said to him, "Give glory to God! First of all, we know this man is a sinner." "I would not know whether he is a sinner or not," he answered. "I know this much: I was blind before; now I can see." They persisted: "Just what did he do to you? How did he open your eyes?" "I have told you once, but you would not listen to me," he answered them. "Why do you want to hear it all over again? Do not tell me you want to become his disciples too?" They retorted scornfully, "You are the one who is that man's disciple. We are disciples of Moses. We

know that God spoke to Moses, but we have no idea where this man comes from." He came back at them: "Well, this is news! You do not know where he comes from, yet he opened my eyes. We know that God does not hear sinners, but that if someone is devout and obeys his will he listens to him. It is unheard of that anyone ever gave sight to a person blind from birth. If this man were not from God, he could never have done such a thing." "What!" they exclaimed, "You are steeped in sin from your birth, and you are giving us lectures?" With that they threw him out bodily.

When Jesus heard of his expulsion, he sought him out and asked him, "Do you believe in the Son of Man?" He answered, "Who is he, sir, that I may believe in him?" "You have seen him," Jesus replied. "He is speaking to you now." ["I do believe, Lord," he said, and bowed down to worship him. Then Jesus said:]

"I came into this world to divide it,
    to make the sightless see
    and the seeing blind."

Some of the Pharisees around him picked this up, saying, "You are not counting us in with the blind, are you?" To which Jesus replied:

"If you were blind
    there would be no sin in that.
    'But we see,' you say,
    and your sin remains."

This is the gospel of the Lord.

7. General Intercessions

The general intercessions (prayer of the faithful) then follow.

(a suggested form)

Invitatory

Because we are a priestly people, "a chosen race, a royal priesthood, a holy nation, a people set apart"—especially when Christ has gathered us together—let us unite now with one another, and as one with Christ exercise our priesthood to pray for today's needs in the Church and in the world.

Petitions

For the leaders of Church and State, religion and government that the Spirit may enlighten them to see what is right and good for those they lead . . .

For the heads of communities, institutions, homes and households that they may be guided by the Spirit in the search for peace and order, freedom and brotherly love among the members of their families . . .

For husbands and wives, fathers and mothers that they will turn to Christ for help in making those crucial decisions which affect the next generation . . .

For young people, that the light of Christ may shine for them in the midst of a confused today and an uncertain tomorrow . . .

For children that they may grow up blessed with those things of the world which will unfold their innermost selves toward the eternal light of the Spirit . . .

For all dedicated single people . . .

For all lonely and alienated people . . .

For all poor and hungry people . . .

For all people sick in body, mind, or spirit . . .

For all those around us, for those we know, and for those who need our prayers . . .

For each of us himself, as ever the worst sinner of all . . .

For our relatives, friends, and fellow parishioners who have died . . .

For all mankind, living and dead . . .

Prayer

You are a mighty God, O Lord, who can help us all; you are a knowing God who knows better than ourselves what we need; you are a compassionate Father who wants to be good to us; you are a faithful God who keeps his promises; you are a generous God who has promised to give us "good measure, pressed down, shaken together, and running over." Your name be praised for ever and ever! Amen.

PRAYER OF THE FAITHFUL

What is uppermost in your thoughts when you get yourself together before the Lord? Family or personal troubles or hopes? A sick relative? Your own inarticulate longings for the simple presence of God, for a personal understanding of his word, for knowledge of his will and for the capacity to hear and obey him? Your list is probably quite standard.

The point is, is your prayer a prayer of faith, or is it merely a litany, asking God for favors? Do you pray with confidence, or do you utter only a self-centered cry?

Recently "prayer of petition" has fallen into some disfavor. It is said that our prayer should be more than "gimme," and of course it should. But an authority above all spiritual masters tells us: "Ask, and you shall receive." A wise man has said that all prayer, even that of adoration, reparation, and thanksgiving, is really basically prayer of petition. In every prayer, particularly the asking one, we recognize God's power and mercy, we express our confidence in the one who can do something to help us. Which is really to let God be God.

But there is more behind the feeling about petitionary prayer. The danger is to think that once we have prayed, our task is finished. We sit back and wait for something to happen.

If we can do something about our situation, obviously we must. And, if we examine ourselves truthfully, we know that we can do *something* about most any problem, at least we can change our attitude toward it. To pray with faith is to *be* faithful.

Do you pray for peace in the family? In the world? Begin also to work for it. Prayer doesn't change God. Prayer changes us. If we really pray, God will give us the heart to change, or to bear what we cannot change.

WE PRAY FOR OURSELVES

The time has come for the people to pray for the people of God. Unabashedly, we now pray a prayer of petition.

That all may be well with the big men of the Church . . . That all may be well with the big men of the State . . . for together these two are as big as life, affecting all our lives.

They exist for man, inevitably religious and social, who forever needs the organization, initiative, and leadership that makes community possible — mankind working together, the brotherhood of man.

That all people everywhere: black men and white men and yellow men and brown men and red men . . . the rich, the poor and the middle class . . . the overfed and the starving . . . the naked and the multiwardrobed—that each be blessed according to his peculiar need.

That our city, our town, our parish community . . . that this assembly of people who have come together . . . that our friends, brothers and sisters, parents, living and dead, may all be well.

And me too, Lord, give me what I need.

7. Life for Lazarus

*(From the Liturgy of the Word for the
FIFTH SUNDAY OF LENT)*   **A**

READING I   **Ez 37:12-14**

A reading from the book of the prophet Ezekiel
I shall put my spirit in you, and you will live.

Thus says the Lord God: O my people, I will
open your graves and have you rise from them,
and bring you back to the land of Israel. Then
you shall know that I am the Lord, when I open
your graves and have you rise from them, O my
people! I will put my spirit in you that you may
live, and I will settle you upon your land; thus
you shall know that I am the Lord. I have promised, and I will do it, says the Lord.

This is the Word of the Lord.

Responsorial Psalm   Ps 130:1-2, 3-4, 5-6, 7-8

R. *(7) With the Lord there is mercy, and fullness of redemption.*

Out of the depths I cry to you, O Lord;
  Lord, hear my voice!
Let your ears be attentive
  to my voice in supplication.

R. *With the Lord there is mercy, and fullness
of redemption.*

If you, O Lord, mark iniquities,
  Lord, who can stand?
But with you is forgiveness,
  that you may be revered.

R. *With the Lord there is mercy, and fullness
of redemption.*

I trust in the Lord;
  my soul trusts in his word.
More than sentinels wait for the dawn,
  let Israel wait for the Lord.

R. *With the Lord there is mercy, and fullness
of redemption.*

For with the Lord is kindness
  and with him is plenteous redemption;
And he will redeem Israel
  from all their iniquities.

R. *With the Lord there is mercy, and fullness
of redemption.*

READING II   **Rom 8:8-11**

A reading from the letter of Paul to the Romans
If the Spirit of him who raised Jesus from the dead is living
in you then he will give life to your own mortal bodies.

Those who are in the flesh cannot please God.
But you are not in the flesh; you are in the spirit,
since the Spirit of God dwells in you. If anyone
does not have the Spirit of Christ, he does not
belong to Christ. If Christ is in you, the body is
indeed dead because of sin, while the spirit lives
because of justice. If the Spirit of him who raised
Jesus from the dead dwells in you, then he who
raised Christ from the dead will bring your mortal
bodies to life also through his Spirit dwelling in
you.

This is the Word of the Lord.

GOSPEL

Jn 11:1-45

Verse before the Gospel   Jn 11:25-26

I am the resurrection and the life, said the Lord:
he who believes in me will not die for ever.

✠ *A reading from the holy gospel according to
John*
I am the resurrection and the life.

There was a certain man named Lazarus who
was sick. He was from Bethany, the village of
Mary and her sister Martha. (This Mary whose
brother Lazarus was sick was the one who
anointed the Lord with perfume and dried his
feet with her hair.) The sisters sent word to Jesus
to inform him, "Lord, the one you love is sick."
Upon hearing this, Jesus said:

"This sickness is not to end in death; rather it
is for God's glory,
that through it the Son of God may be glorified."

Jesus loved Martha and her sister and Lazarus
very much. Yet, after hearing that Lazarus was
sick, he stayed on where he was for two days
more. Finally he said to his disciples, "Let us go
back to Judea." "Rabbi," protested the disciples,
"with the Jews only recently trying to stone you,
you are going back up there again?" Jesus answered:

"Are there not twelve hours of daylight?
If a man goes walking by day he does not
stumble,
because he sees the world bathed in light.
But if he goes walking at night he will stumble,
since there is no light in him."

After uttering these words, he added, "Our beloved Lazarus has fallen asleep, but I am going
there to wake him." At this the disciples objected,
"Lord, if he is asleep his life will be saved." Jesus
had been speaking about his death, but they
thought he meant sleep in the sense of slumber.
Finally Jesus said plainly, "Lazarus is dead. For
your sakes I am glad I was not there, that you
may come to believe. In any event, let us go to
him." Then Thomas (the name means "Twin")
said to his fellow disciples, "Let us go along, to
die with him."

When Jesus arrived at Bethany, he found that
Lazarus had already been in the tomb four days.
The village was not far from Jerusalem—just under two miles—and many Jewish people had
come out to console Martha and Mary over their
brother. When Martha heard that Jesus was coming she went to meet him, while Mary sat at
home. Martha said to Jesus, "Lord, if you had
been here, my brother would never have died.
Even now, I am sure that God will give you
whatever you ask of him." "Your brother will rise
again," Jesus assured her. "I know he will rise
again," Martha replied, "in the resurrection on
the last day." Jesus told her:

"I am the resurrection and the life:
whoever believes in me,
though he should die, will come to life; and
whoever is alive and believes in me will
never die.

Do you believe this?" "Yes, Lord," she replied.
"I have come to believe that you are the Messiah,
the Son of God: he who is to come into the
world."

When she had said this she went back and
called her sister Mary. "The Teacher is here, asking for you," she whispered. As soon as Mary
heard this, she got up and started out in his direction. (Actually Jesus had not yet come into the

village but was still at the spot where Martha had met him.) The Jews who were in the house with Mary consoling her saw her get up quickly and go out, so they followed her, thinking she was going to the tomb to weep there. When Mary came to the place where Jesus was, seeing him, she fell at his feet and said to him, "Lord, if you had been here my brother would never have died." When Jesus saw her weeping, and the Jewish folk who had accompanied her also weeping, he was troubled in spirit, moved by the deepest emotions. "Where have you laid him?" he asked. "Lord, come and see," they said. Jesus began to weep, which caused the Jews to remark, "See how much he loved him!" But some said, "He opened the eyes of that blind man. Why could he not have done something to stop this man from dying?" Once again troubled in spirit, Jesus approached the tomb.

It was a cave with a stone laid across it. "Take away the stone," Jesus directed. Martha, the dead man's sister, said to him, "Lord, it has been four days now; surely there will be a stench!" Jesus replied, "Did I not assure you that if you believed you would see the glory of God?" They then took away the stone and Jesus looked upward and said:

"Father, I thank you for having heard me.

I know that you always hear me

but I have said this for the sake of the crowd,

that they may believe that you sent me."

Having said this, he called loudly, "Lazarus, come out!" The dead man came out, bound hand and foot with linen strips, his face wrapped in a cloth. "Untie him," Jesus told them, "and let him go free."

This caused many of the Jews who had come to visit Mary, and had seen what Jesus did, to put their faith in him.

This is the gospel of the Lord.

PART 3

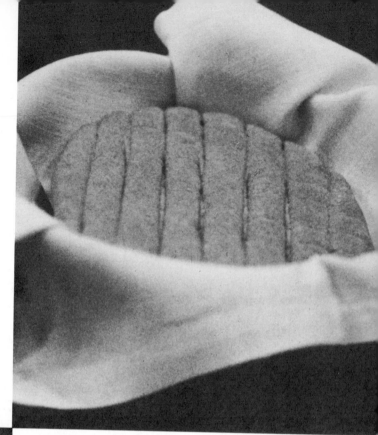

Liturgy of the Eucharist

PREPARATION OF GIFTS

8. The Gifts of Bread and Wine

The offertory song is begun, and the altar is prepared, and the people bring the gifts to the altar.

It is desirable that the participation of the faithful be expressed by members of the congregation bringing up the bread and wine for the celebration of the Eucharist or other gifts for the needs of the Church and the poor.

FAITHFUL BRING UP GIFTS

A family, or a representative grouping of different elements in the congregation, brings up the bread and wine. People of all types and classes offer gifts. What better symbolic action than God's people moving forward to his altar, their hands bearing fruits of their common existence.

Bread and wine represent us . . . our work, our lives, all that we are and have. People in some parishes bring up gifts for the poor.

Having ushers bring up the collection at this time is also a significant gesture. It is a way of calling attention to an important fact of existence today, namely, that our money too represents us, our labor, our sacrifices, our human efforts, our very lives.

Is our concern the family? The poor? Equal housing? Equal opportunity in jobs? Education? Family assistance? Peace? It's all going to take money . . . our own and other people's. We have to tighten our belts, to live more simply, to give . . . that everybody may have some.

We should all contribute something as we offer our gifts now, so that all can participate with dignity at the banquet table.

BREAD AND WINE

In coming to Mass, we have come to a celebration different from any other celebration. It is a highly ritualized celebration because only by means of sign and symbol can all the unseen richness of its reality be even obscurely expressed.

We are celebrating Christ, great mystery and great sacrament, in the way he asked us to. We are celebrating Christ with a sacrificial meal, not with a big meal with much to eat and drink, but with a meal like the Last Supper, where there was the coming together of Christ's friends, communication, and love—above all, the love of the One who was going to die for the others tomorrow.

Along with Christ, we are celebrating all those who together with Christ died yesterday and will live and die today and tomorrow—like him for others. We enter into this celebration completely only if we can count ourselves among the Christs of tomorrow.

The sign for this celebration of love, of life-and-death love, is bread and wine—classical symbols of food and drink, of nourishment and exhilaration, of life from death, of body and blood.

We the people bring up the bread and wine now, sign of ourselves to be made into a sign of Christ.

8. The Lord's Supper

*(From the Liturgy of the Word for
HOLY THURSDAY)* **A B C**

READING I Ex 12:1-8, 11-14

A reading from the book of Exodus
The law for the passover meal.

The Lord said to Moses and Aaron in the land of Egypt, "This month shall stand at the head of your calendar; you shall reckon it the first month of the year. Tell the whole community of Israel: On the tenth of this month every one of your families must procure for itself a lamb, one apiece for each household. If a family is too small for a whole lamb, it shall join the nearest household in procuring one and shall share in the lamb in proportion to the number of persons who partake of it. The lamb must be a year-old male and without blemish. You may take it from either the sheep or the goats. You shall keep it until the fourteenth day of this month, and then, with the whole assembly of Israel present, it shall be slaughtered during the evening twilight. They shall take some of its blood and apply it to the two doorposts and the lintel of every house in which they partake of the lamb. That same night they shall eat its roasted flesh with unleavened bread and bitter herbs.

"This is how you are to eat it: with your loins girt, sandals on your feet and your staff in hand, you shall eat like those who are in flight. It is the Passover of the Lord. For on this same night I will go through Egypt, striking down every firstborn of the land, both man and beast, and executing judgment on all the gods of Egypt—I, the Lord! But the blood will mark the houses where you are. Seeing the blood, I will pass over you; thus, when I strike the land of Egypt, no destructive blow will come upon you.

"This day shall be a memorial feast for you, which all your generations shall celebrate with pilgrimage to the Lord, as a perpetual institution."

This is the Word of the Lord.

Responsorial Psalm Ps 116:12-13, 15-16, 17-18

R. *(See 1 Cor 10:16) Our blessing-cup is a communion with the blood of Christ.*

How shall I make a return to the Lord
  for all the good he has done for me?
The cup of salvation I will take up,
  and I will call upon the name of the Lord.

R. *Our blessing-cup is a communion with the blood of Christ.*

Precious in the eyes of the Lord
  is the death of his faithful ones.
I am your servant, the son of your handmaid;
  you have loosed my bonds.

R. *Our blessing-cup is a communion with the blood of Christ.*

To you will I offer sacrifice of thanksgiving,
  and I will call upon the name of the Lord.
My vows to the Lord I will pay
  in the presence of all his people.

R. *Our blessing-cup is a communion with the blood of Christ.*

READING II

1 Cor 11:23-26

A reading from the first letter of Paul to the Corinthians
Until the Lord comes, every time you eat this bread and drink this cup, you proclaim his death.

I received from the Lord what I handed on to you, namely, that the Lord Jesus on the night in which he was betrayed took bread, and after he had given thanks, broke it and said, "This is my body, which is for you. Do this in remembrance of me." In the same way, after the supper, he took the cup, saying, "This cup is the new covenant in my blood. Do this, whenever you drink it, in remembrance of me." Every time, then, you eat this bread and drink this cup, you proclaim the death of the Lord until he comes!

This is the Word of the Lord.

GOSPEL

Jn 13:1-15

Verse before the Gospel   Jn 13:34

I give you a new commandment:
    love one another as I have loved you.

✠ *A reading from the holy gospel according to John*
Now he showed how perfect was his love.

Before the feast of Passover, Jesus realized that the hour had come for him to pass from this world to the Father. He had loved his own in this world, and would show his love for them to the end. The devil had already induced Judas, son of Simon Iscariot, to hand Jesus over; and so, during the supper, Jesus—fully aware that he had come from God and was going to God, the Father who had handed everything over to him—rose from the meal and took off his cloak. He picked up a towel and tied it around himself. Then he poured water into a basin and began to wash his disciples' feet and dry them with the towel he had around him. Thus he came to Simon Peter, who said to him, "Lord, are you going to wash my feet?" Jesus answered, "You may not realize now what I am doing, but later you will understand." Peter replied, "You shall never wash my feet!" "If I do not wash you," Jesus answered, "you will have no share in my heritage." "Lord," Simon Peter said to him, "then not only my feet, but my hands and head as well." Jesus told him, "The man who has bathed has no need to wash [except for his feet]; he is entirely cleansed, just as you are; though not all." (The reason he said, "Not all are washed clean," was that he knew his betrayer.)

After he had washed their feet, he put his cloak back on and reclined at table once more. He said to them:
    "Do you understand what I just did for you?
    You address me as 'Teacher' and 'Lord,'
        and fittingly enough,
        for that is what I am.
    But if I washed your feet—
        I who am Teacher and Lord—
        then you must wash each other's feet.
    What I just did was to give you an example:
        as I have done, so you must do."

This is the gospel of the Lord.

9. Offering of the Gifts

Priest: Blessed are you, Lord, God of all creation. Through your goodness we have
this bread to offer, which earth has
given and human hands have made. It
will become for us the bread of life.

If no song is sung, the people respond:

People: Blessed be God for ever.

While pouring water into the chalice:

Priest: By the mystery of this water and wine
may we come to share in the divinity
of Christ, who humbled himself to share
in our humanity.

Priest: Blessed are you, Lord, God of all creation. Through your goodness we have
this wine to offer, fruit of the vine and
work of human hands. It will become
our spiritual drink.

If no song is sung, the people respond:

People: Blessed be God for ever.

Priest: Lord God, we ask you to receive us and
be pleased with the sacrifice we offer
you with humble and contrite hearts.

*Washing his hands, the priest says
quietly:*

Priest: Lord, wash away my iniquity; cleanse
me from my sin.

THROUGH OUR PRIEST

The priest offers our gifts. Called by God, chosen from among the people, he stands for the people before the Lord.

The whole idea is archaic, some say. Ours is the day of the direct approach. We get what we want by going directly to the head man. No mediators need apply. We can dispense with priests, with vestment and ritual.

Furthermore, the argument goes, the gospel speaks first of poverty and active charity, of worshiping "in spirit and in truth." Why this liturgy which speaks of gifts, obligations, sacrifice, and even richness? Why this waste of purely symbolic human effort?

The argument deceives.

We may rightly question the efficacy of ritual alone to nourish the life of today's Christian: there is no scene more devoid of true religion than the pious on Sunday turning into the impious on Monday . . . or even in the parking lot on Sunday.

But it would be supreme presumption to attempt to raise ourselves above the common condition of man, to think that we can dispense with his need to use sign and symbol to express the mystery of his relationship with God.

From the beginning man has presented gifts to his God, to solicit his help, to express his complete dependence. And between man and God were always the priest and the altar. Not as a block or barrier, but as a facilitator of communication. Not as something between, but a link with.

Jesus was the only one to stand before the Father without mediator. He took upon himself the burden of facing the unfaceable.

Yes, we have in God a Father, one who is loving kindness itself. But we need Jesus to reveal him to us. It is he who takes the gifts we offer through our priest and presents them to the Father of us all. It is he who shows us how graciously they are received.

WORK OF HUMAN HANDS

The bread and wine which the people have brought up are the work of human hands. Human hands have raised the wheat. Human hands have planted the grapes. Seeds have fulfilled their promises.

Producing bread from wheat is also a labor of hands, and wine from grapes a yet longer labor. The wheat gets ground and the grapes get crushed in the process to make something new. The new is something made out of the good things of earth. It is already a mixture of what man has given and God has given. Always God and man are mixed up together.

We take what man has made and we offer it. Sometimes we ourselves have made this very bread and wine. Or we *might* have made it. It is a familiar process and we are able to identify ourselves with it.

But we can also identify God with it. He made the first move, and the second. He created the earth-potential for wheat and grape; he created us makers in his image.

We ask now that Christ join himself to our offering. He is his Father's son and son of man. He is our one big brother, our true image before God.

9. Passion and Death of Jesus

(From the Liturgy of the Word for
GOOD FRIDAY) **A B C**

READING I   Is 52:13-53, 12

A reading from the book of the prophet Isaiah
He surrendered himself to death, while bearing the faults of
many (Fourth song of the Servant of Yahweh).

See, my servant shall prosper,
   he shall be raised high and greatly exalted.
Even as many were amazed at him—
   so marred was his look beyond that of man,
   and his appearance beyond that of mortals—
So shall he startle many nations,
   because of him kings shall stand speechless;
For those who have not been told shall see,
   those who have not heard shall ponder it.

Who would believe what we have heard?
   To whom has the arm of the Lord been re-
      vealed?
He grew up like a sapling before him,
   like a shoot from the parched earth;
There was in him no stately bearing to make us
      look at him,
   nor appearance that would attract us to him.
He was spurned and avoided by men,
   a man of suffering, accustomed to infirmity,
One of those from whom men hide their faces,
   spurned, and we held him in no esteem.

Yet it was our infirmities that he bore,
   our sufferings that he endured,
While we thought of him as stricken,
   as one smitten by God and afflicted.
But he was pierced for our offenses,
   crushed for our sins;
Upon him was the chastisement that makes us
      whole,
   by his stripes we were healed.
We had all gone astray like sheep,
each following his own way;
But the Lord laid upon him
   the guilt of us all.

Though he was harshly treated, he submitted
   and opened not his mouth;
Like a lamb led to the slaughter
   or a sheep before the shearers,
   he was silent and opened not his mouth.
Oppressed and condemned, he was taken away,
   and who would have thought any more of his
      destiny?
When he was cut off from the land of the living,
   and smitten for the sin of his people,
A grave was assigned him among the wicked
   and a burial place with evildoers,
Though he had done no wrong
   nor spoken any falsehood.
[But the Lord was pleased
   to crush him in infirmity.]

If he gives his life as an offering for sin,
   he shall see his descendants in a long life,
   and the will of the Lord shall be accomplished
      through him.
Because of his affliction
   he shall see the light in fullness of days;
Through his suffering, my servant shall justify
      many,
   and their guilt he shall bear.
Therefore I will give him his portion among the
      great,
   and he shall divide the spoils with the mighty,
Because he surrendered himself to death
   and was counted among the wicked;
And he shall take away the sins of many,
   and win pardon for their offenses.

This is the Word of the Lord.

Responsorial Psalm Ps 31:2, 6, 12-13, 15-16, 17, 25

R.   (Lk 23:46) *Father, I put my life in your hands.*

In you, O Lord, I take refuge;
   let me never be put to shame.
   In your justice rescue me.
Into your hands I commend my spirit;
   you will redeem me, O Lord, O faithful God.

R.   *Father, I put my life in your hands.*

For all my foes I am an object of reproach,
   a laughingstock to my neighbors, and a dread
      to my friends;
   they who see me abroad flee from me.
I am forgotten like the unremembered dead;
   I am like a dish that is broken.

R.   *Father, I put my life in your hands.*

But my trust is in you, O Lord;
   I say, "You are my God."
In your hands is my destiny; rescue me
   from the clutches of my enemies and my per-
      secutors.

R.   *Father, I put my life in your hands.*

Let your face shine upon your servant;
   save me in your kindness.
Take courage and be stouthearted,
   all you who hope in the Lord.

R.   *Father, I put my life in your hands.*

READING II   Heb 4:14-16, 5, 7-9

A reading from the letter of Paul to the Hebrews
He submitted humbly and became for all the source of
eternal salvation.

We have a great high priest who has passed through the heavens, Jesus, the Son of God; let us hold fast to our profession of faith. For we do not have a high priest who is unable to sympathize with our weakness, but one who was tempted in every way that we are, yet never sinned. So let us confidently approach the throne of grace to receive mercy and favor and to find help in time of need.

In the days when he was in the flesh, Christ offered prayers and supplications with loud cries and tears to God, who was able to save him from death, and he was heard because of his reverence. Son though he was, he learned obedience from what he suffered; and when perfected, he became the source of eternal salvation for all who obey him.

This is the Word of the Lord.

GOSPEL   Jn 18:1-19:42

Verse before the Gospel   Phil 2:8-9

Christ became obedient for us even to death, dying on the cross.
Therefore God raised him on high
and gave him the name above all other names.

The Passion of our Lord Jesus Christ according to John

Jesus went out with his disciples across the Kidron valley. There was a garden there, and he and his disciples entered it. The place was familiar to Judas as well (the one who was to hand him over) because Jesus had often met there with his disciples. Judas took the cohort as well as police supplied by the chief priests and the Pharisees, and came there with lanterns, torches and weapons. Jesus, aware of all that would happen to him, stepped forward and said to them, "Who is it you want?" "Jesus the Nazorean," they replied. "I am he," he answered. (Now Judas, the one who was to hand him over, was right there with them.) As Jesus said to them, "I am he," they retreated slightly and fell to the ground. Jesus put the question to them again, "Who is it you want?" "Jesus the Nazorean," they repeated. "I have told you, I am he," Jesus said. "If I am the one you want, let these men go." (This was to fulfill what he had said, "I have not lost one of those you gave me.")

Then Simon Peter, who had a sword, drew it and struck the slave of the high priest, severing his right ear. (The slave's name was Malchus.) At that Jesus said to Peter, "Put your sword back in its sheath. Am I not to drink the cup the Father has given me?"

Then the soldiers of the cohort, their tribune, and the Jewish police arrested Jesus and bound him. They led him first to Annas, the father-in-law of Caiaphas who was high priest that year. (It was Caiaphas who had proposed to the Jews the advantage of having one man die for the people.)

Simon Peter, in company with another disciple, kept following Jesus closely. This disciple, who was known to the high priest, stayed with Jesus as far as the high priest's courtyard, while Peter was left standing at the gate. The disciple known to the high priest came out and spoke to the woman at the gate, and then brought Peter in. This servant girl who kept the gate said to Peter, "Aren't you one of this man's followers?" "Not I," he replied.

Now the night was cold, and the servants and the guards who were standing around had made a charcoal fire to warm themselves by. Peter joined them and stood there warming himself.

The high priest questioned Jesus, first about his disciples, then about his teaching. Jesus answered by saying:

"I have spoken publicly to any who would listen.
I always taught in a synagogue or in the temple area
   where all the Jews come together.

There was nothing secret about anything I said. Why do you question me? Question those who heard me when I spoke. It should be obvious they will know what I said." At this reply, one of the guards who was standing nearby gave Jesus a sharp blow on the face. "Is that any way to answer the high priest?" he said. Jesus replied, "If I said anything wrong produce the evidence, but if I spoke the truth why hit me?" Annas next sent him, bound, to the high priest Caiaphas.

All through this, Simon Peter had been standing there warming himself. They said to him, "Are you not a disciple of his?" He denied: "I am not!" "But did I not see you with him in the garden?" insisted one of the high priest's slaves —as it happened, a relative of the man whose ear Peter had severed. Peter denied it again. At that moment a cock began to crow.

At daybreak they brought Jesus from Caiaphas to the praetorium. They did not enter the praetorium themselves, for they had to avoid ritual impurity if they were to eat the Passover supper. Pilate came out to them. "What accusation do you bring against this man?" he demanded. "If he were not a criminal," they retorted, "we would certainly not have handed him over to you." At this Pilate said, "Why do you not take him and pass judgment on him according to your law?" "We may not put anyone to death," the Jews answered. (This was to fulfill what Jesus had said, indicating the sort of death he would die.)

Pilate went back into the praetorium and summoned Jesus. "Are you the King of the Jews?" he asked him. Jesus answered, "Are you saying this on your own, or have others been telling you about me?" "I am no Jew!" Pilate retorted. "It is your own people and the chief priests who have handed you over to me. What have you done?" Jesus answered:
"My kingdom does not belong to this world.
If my kingdom were of this world,
   my subjects would be fighting
      to save me from being handed over to the Jews.
As it is, my kingdom is not here."
At this Pilate said to him, "So, then, you are a king?" Jesus replied:
"It is you who say I am a king.
The reason I was born,
   the reason why I came into the world,
   is to testify to the truth.
Anyone committed to the truth hears my voice."

"Truth!" said Pilate, "What does that mean?"

After this remark, Pilate went out again to the Jews and told them: "Speaking for myself, I find no case against this man. Recall your custom whereby I release to you someone at Passover time. Do you want me to release to you the king of the Jews?" They shouted back, "We want Barabbas, not this one!" (Barabbas was an insurrectionist.)

Pilate's next move was to take Jesus and have him scourged. The soldiers then wove a crown of thorns and fixed it on his head, throwing around his shoulders a cloak of royal purple. Repeatedly they came up to him and said, "All hail, King of the Jews!" slapping his face as they did so.

Pilate went out a second time and said to the crowd: "Observe what I do. I am going to bring him out to you to make you realize that I find no case against him." When Jesus came out wearing the crown of thorns and the purple cloak, Pilate said to them, "Look at the man!" As soon as the chief priests and the temple police saw him they shouted, "Crucify him! Crucify him!" Pilate said, "Take him and crucify him yourselves; I find no case against him." "We have our law," the Jews responded, "and according to that law he must die because he made himself God's Son." When Pilate heard this kind of talk, he was more afraid than ever.

Going back into the praetorium, he said to Jesus, "Where do you come from?" Jesus would not give him any answer. "Do you refuse to speak to me?" Pilate asked him. "Do you not know that I have the power to release you and the power to crucify you?" Jesus answered:

"You would have no power over me whatever unless it were given you from above.
That is why he who handed me over to you is guilty of the greater sin."

After this, Pilate was eager to release him, but the Jews shouted, "If you free this man you are no 'Friend of Caesar.' Anyone who makes himself a king becomes Caesar's rival." Pilate heard what they were saying, then brought Jesus outside and took a seat on a judge's bench at the place called the Stone Pavement—*Gabbatha* in Hebrew. (It was the Preparation Day for Passover, and the hour was about noon.) He said to the Jews, "Look at your king!" At this they shouted, "Away with him! Away with him! Crucify him!" "What!" Pilate exclaimed. "Shall I crucify your king?" The chief priests replied, "We have no king but Caesar." In the end, Pilate handed Jesus over to be crucified.

Jesus was led away, and carrying the cross by himself, went out to what is called the Place of the Skull (in Hebrew, *Golgotha).* There they crucified him, and two others with him: one on either side, Jesus in the middle. Pilate had an inscription placed on the cross which read,

JESUS THE NAZOREAN
THE KING OF THE JEWS

This inscription, in Hebrew, Latin and Greek, was read by many of the Jews, since the place where Jesus was crucified was near the city. The chief priests of the Jews tried to tell Pilate, "You should not have written, 'The King of the Jews.' Write instead, 'This man claimed to be king of the Jews.' " Pilate answered, "What I have written, I have written."

After the soldiers had crucified Jesus they took his garments and divided them four ways, one for each soldier. There was also his tunic, but this tunic was woven in one piece from top to bottom and had no seam. They said to each other, "We shouldn't tear it. Let's throw dice to see who gets it." (The purpose of this was to have the Scripture fulfilled:

"They divided my garments among them; for my clothing they cast lots.")

And this was what the soldiers did.

Near the cross of Jesus there stood his mother, his mother's sister, Mary the wife of Clopas, and Mary Magdalene. Seeing his mother there with the disciple whom he loved, Jesus said to his mother, "Woman, there is your son." In turn he said to the disciple, "There is your mother." From that hour onward, the disciple took her into his care.

After that, Jesus, realizing that everything was now finished, to bring the Scripture to fulfillment said, "I am thirsty." There was a jar there, full of common wine. They stuck a sponge soaked in this wine on some hyssop and raised it to his lips. When Jesus took the wine, he said, "Now it is finished." Then he bowed his head, and delivered over his spirit.

Since it was the Preparation Day the Jews did not want to have the bodies left on the cross during the sabbath, for that sabbath was a solemn feast day. They asked Pilate that the legs be broken and the bodies be taken away. Accordingly, the soldiers came and broke the legs of the men crucified with Jesus, first of one, then of the other. When they came to Jesus and saw that he was already dead, they did not break his legs. One of the soldiers ran a lance into his side, and immediately blood and water flowed out. (This testimony has been given by an eyewitness, and his testimony is true. He tells what he knows is true, so that you may believe.) These events took place for the fulfillment of Scripture:

"Break none of his bones."

There is still another Scripture passage which says:

"They shall look on him whom they have pierced."

Afterward, Joseph of Arimathea, a disciple of Jesus (although a secret one for fear of the Jews), asked Pilate's permission to remove Jesus' body. Pilate granted it, so they came and took the body away. Nicodemus (the man who had first come to Jesus at night) likewise came, bringing a mixture of myrrh and aloes which weighed about a hundred pounds. They took Jesus' body, and in accordance with Jewish burial custom bound it up in wrappings of cloth with perfumed oils. In the place where he had been crucified there was a garden, and in the garden a new tomb in which no one had ever been laid. Because of the Jewish Preparation Day they laid Jesus there, for the tomb was close at hand.

This is the gospel of the Lord.

10. Your Sacrifice and Mine

Then to the people:

Priest: Pray, brethren, that our sacrifice may be acceptable to God, the almighty Father.

People: May the Lord accept the sacrifice at your hands
for the praise and glory of his name,
for our good, and the good of all his Church.

The prayer over the gifts follows; the people respond:

People: Amen.

OUR SACRIFICE

Up to this point in the Mass ritual there has been little mention of sacrifice. Here priest and people together, as representatives of all humanity, offer gifts of "sacrifice." It is the supreme act of religion.

For all its hallowed tradition, however, the notion of sacrifice can be misunderstood. The word conjures up images of occult rites and tribal blood offerings.

We offer sacrifice, yes, but not as the pagans of old. They offered their victims to appease an angry god, or to exercise some kind of hold on his power. We have also gone beyond the bloody sacrifices and burnt offerings of the Old Law.

Our sacrifice is Christ's sacrifice: his body and blood offered up to save us and offered to us as food: sacramental food, sacramental sacrifice. Our sacrifice is a sacrifice of worship, a "clean oblation," the sacrifice of the new covenant. Our offering is Christ, the true worshiper:

"Sacrifice and oblation you did not want, but a body you prepared for me: In holocausts and sin-offerings you had no pleasure. Then said I, 'Behold, I come to do your will, O God.'"

What we come to Mass to offer is Christ, along with ourselves: all that we are and have and will ever be. When we offer our gifts we affirm that God is good and great and full of loving-kindness. We confirm that life, in spite of all, is good . . . that because of Christ, all life is sacred, fit for giving, supremely suitable for celebration. All has been graced with God's presence and power.

Not everything in life, obviously, is immediately ready for offering. Making the world holy does not happen without its participating in sacrifice. The Incarnation at present is in process, as yet incomplete. It will come to its fullness only with much effort directed and sustained by the power of God in Christ. The process is a fumbling one, full of failure. Our contribution entails suffering and setback. But with Paul we can say: We "fill up what is lacking in the sufferings of Christ."

PRAY, BRETHREN

Bread and wine, work of human hands, have been offered in prayer by the priest. What man has made ready for the feast has been offered to God.

The priest faces the people to talk with them. He wants the people to ratify his prayer with theirs. He initiates an exchange about what he has done. We are together in this, he says; You pray too.

We pray that *our* sacrifice may be acceptable. It will be acceptable when we make it Christ's too. His was the perfect sacrifice, the sacrifice to end all other sacrifices. From now on it is a matter of keeping going and of renewing the sacrifice of Christ. All our preparation and getting ready is to join our sacrifice with his, himself with us.

We are acceptable in the measure Christ can identify with us. Our sacrifice will be acceptable in the measure it can be identified with his.

10. The Resurrection of the Lord

(From the Liturgy of the Word for the EASTER VIGIL) **A B C**

READING I   Ex 14:15 - 15:1

A reading from the book of Exodus
Tell the sons of Israel to march on, to walk through the
sea on dry ground.

The Lord said to Moses, "Why are you crying out to me? Tell the Israelites to go forward. And you, lift up your staff and, with hand outstretched over the sea, split the sea in two, that the Israelites may pass through it on dry land. But I will make the Egyptians so obstinate that they will go in after them. Then I will receive glory through Pharaoh and all his army, his chariots and charioteers. The Egyptians shall know that I am the Lord, when I receive glory through Pharaoh and his chariots and charioteers."

The angel of God, who had been leading Israel's camp, now moved and went around behind them. The column of cloud also, leaving the front, took up its place behind them, so that it came between the camp of the Egyptians and that of Israel. But the cloud now became dark, and thus the night passed without the rival camps coming any closer together all night long. Then Moses stretched out his hand over the sea, and the Lord swept the sea with a strong east wind throughout the night and so turned it into dry land. When the water was thus divided, the Israelites marched into the midst of the sea on dry land, with the water like a wall to their right and to their left.

The Egyptians followed in pursuit; all Pharaoh's horses and chariots and charioteers went after them right into the midst of the sea. In the night watch just before dawn the Lord cast through the column of the fiery cloud upon the Egyptian force a glance that threw it into a panic; and he so clogged their chariot wheels that they could hardly drive. With that the Egyptians sounded the retreat before Israel, because the Lord was fighting for them against the Egyptians.

Then the Lord told Moses, "Stretch out your hand over the sea, that the water may flow back upon the Egyptians, upon their chariots and their charioteers." So Moses stretched out his hand over the sea, and at dawn the sea flowed back to its normal depth. The Egyptians were fleeing head on toward the sea, when the Lord hurled them into its midst. As the water flowed back, it covered the chariots and the charioteers of Pharaoh's whole army which had followed the Israelites into the sea. Not a single one of them escaped. But the Israelites had marched on dry land through the midst of the sea, with the water like a wall to their right and to their left. Thus the Lord saved Israel on that day from the power of the Egyptians. When Israel saw the Egyptians lying dead on the seashore and beheld the great power that the Lord had shown against the Egyptians, they feared the Lord and believed in him and in his servant Moses.

Then Moses and the Israelites sang this song to the Lord:

I will sing to the Lord, for he is gloriously triumphant;
> horse and chariot he has cast into the sea.

This is the Word of the Lord.

Responsorial Psalm Ex 15:1-2, 3-4, 5-6, 17-18

R. *(1) Let us sing to the Lord; he has covered himself in glory.*

I will sing to the Lord, for he is gloriously triumphant;
   horse and chariot he has cast into the sea.
My strength and my courage is the Lord,
   and he has been my savior.
He is my God, I praise him;
   the God of my father, I extol him.

R. *Let us sing to the Lord; he has covered himself in glory.*

The Lord is a warrior,
   Lord is his name!
Pharaoh's chariots and army he hurled into the sea;
   the elite of his officers were submerged in the Red Sea.

R. *Let us sing to the Lord; he has covered himself in glory.*

The flood waters covered them,
   they sank into the depths like a stone.
Your right hand, O Lord, magnificent in power,
   your right hand, O Lord, has shattered the enemy.

R. *Let us sing to the Lord; he has covered himself in glory.*

You brought in the people you redeemed
   and planted them on the mountain of your inheritance.
The place where you made your seat, O Lord,
   the sanctuary, O Lord, which your hands established.
The Lord shall reign forever and ever.

R. *Let us sing to the Lord; he has covered himself in glory.*

READING II Rom 6:3-11

A reading from the letter of Paul to the Romans
Christ, having been raised from the dead,
will never die again.

Are you not aware that we who were baptized into Christ Jesus were baptized into his death? Through baptism into his death we were buried with him, so that, just as Christ was raised from the dead by the glory of the Father, we too might live a new life. If we have been united with him through likeness to his death, so shall we be through a like resurrection. This we know; our old self was crucified with him so that the sinful body might be destroyed and we might be slaves to sin no longer. A man who is dead has been freed from sin. If we have died with Christ, we believe that we are also to live with him. We know that Christ, once raised from the dead, will never die again; death has no more power over him. His death was death to sin, once for all; his life is life for God. In the same way, you must consider yourselves dead to sin but alive for God in Christ Jesus.

This is the Word of the Lord.

Responsorial Psalm   Ps 118:1-2, 16, 17, 22-23

R.   *Alleluia. Alleluia. Alleluia.*

Give thanks to the Lord, for he is good,
    for his mercy endures forever.
Let the house of Israel say,
    "His mercy endures forever."

R.   *Alleluia. Alleluia. Alleluia.*

The right hand of the Lord has struck with power;
    the right hand of the Lord is exalted.
I shall not die, but live,
    and declare the works of the Lord.

R.   *Alleluia. Alleluia. Alleluia.*

The stone which the builders rejected
    has become the cornerstone.
By the Lord has this been done;
    It is wonderful in our eyes.

R.   *Alleluia. Alleluia. Alleluia.*

GOSPEL A   Mt 28:1-10

✛ *A reading from the holy gospel according to Matthew*
He has risen from the dead and now he is going before
you to Galilee.

After the sabbath, as the first day of the week
was dawning, Mary Magdalene came with the
other Mary to inspect the tomb. Suddenly there
was a mighty earthquake, as the angel of the
Lord descended from heaven. He came to the
stone, rolled it back, and sat on it. In appearance
he resembled a flash of lightning while his garments were as dazzling as snow. The guards grew

paralyzed with fear of him and fell down like dead men. Then the angel spoke, addressing the women: "Do not be frightened. I know you are looking for Jesus the crucified, but he is not here. He has been raised, exactly as he promised. Come and see the spot where he was laid. Then go quickly and tell his disciples: 'He has been raised from the dead and now goes ahead of you to Galilee, where you will see him.' That is the message I have for you."

They hurried away from the tomb half-overjoyed, half-fearful, and ran to carry the good news to his disciples. Suddenly, without warning, Jesus stood before them and said, "Peace!" The women came up and embraced his feet and did him homage. At this Jesus said to them, "Do not be afraid! Go and carry the news to my brothers that they are to go to Galilee, where they will see me."

GOSPEL B   Mk 16:1-8

✛ A reading from the holy gospel according to
Mark
Jesus of Nazareth, who was crucified, has risen.

When the sabbath was over, Mary Magdalene, Mary the mother of James, and Salome bought perfumed oils with which they intended to go and anoint Jesus. Very early, just after sunrise, on the first day of the week they came to the tomb. They were saying to one another, "Who will roll back the stone for us from the entrance to the tomb?" When they looked, they found that the stone had been rolled back. (It was a huge one.) On entering the tomb they saw a young man sitting at the right, dressed in a white robe. This frightened them thoroughly, but he reassured them: "You need not be amazed! You are looking for Jesus of Nazareth, the one who was crucified. He has

been raised up; he is not here. See the place where they laid him. Go now and tell his disciples and Peter, 'He is going ahead of you to Galilee, where you will see him just as he told you.'" They made their way out and fled from the tomb bewildered and trembling; and because of their great fear, they said nothing to anyone.

GOSPEL C   Lk 24:1-12

✛ A reading from the holy gospel according to
Luke
Why look among the dead for someone who is alive?

On the first day of the week, at dawn, the women came to the tomb bringing the spices they had prepared. They found the stone rolled back from the tomb; but when they entered the tomb, they did not find the body of the Lord Jesus. While they were still at a loss what to think of this, two men in dazzling garments appeared beside them. Terrified, the women bowed to the ground. The men said to them: "Why do you search for the living One among the dead? He is not here; he has been raised up. Remember what he said to you while he was still in Galilee—that the Son of Man must be delivered into the hands of sinful men, and be crucified, and on the third day rise again." With this reminder, his words came back to them.

On their return from the tomb, they told all these things to the Eleven and the others. The women were Mary of Magdala, Joanna, and Mary the mother of James. The other women with them also told the apostles, but the story seemed like nonsense and they refused to believe them. Peter, however, got up and ran to the tomb. He stooped down but could see nothing but the wrappings. So he went away full of amazement at what had occurred.

This is the gospel of the Lord.

THE EUCHARISTIC PRAYER

11. Preface of Praise

Priest: The Lord be with you.
People: And also with you.

Priest: Lift up your hearts.
People: We lift them up to the Lord.

Priest: Let us give thanks to the Lord our God.
People: It is right to give him thanks and praise.

Priest: Father in heaven, it is right that we
should give you thanks and glory:
you alone are God, living and true.
Through all eternity you live in unap-
proachable light.
Source of life and goodness, you have
created all things, to fill your creatures
with every blessing
and lead all men to the joyful vision of
your light.
Countless hosts of angels stand before
you to do your will;
they look upon your splendor
and praise you, night and day.
United with them, and in the name of
every creature under heaven,
we too praise your glory as we sing
(say):

All: Holy, holy, holy Lord, God of power
and might,
heaven and earth are full of your glory.
Hosanna in the highest.
Blessed is he who comes in the name
of the Lord.
Hosanna in the highest.

PRAISE OF GOD

(From the "Praise of God" on this page through the "Doxology" on page 103, this column follows through as an expanded Eucharistic Prayer. It is an improvised form by way of explanation.)

Friends and neighbors
brothers and sisters in Christ Jesus
we have arrived at this point in our lives
and at this point in our celebration
through the love of God our Father.
He is our God who
continually creates us anew.
Through his Son he has brought us together
and his Spirit is present among us.

Let us begin our praise of God
by recalling how in the beginning
the Spirit of God
hovered over the veil of nothingness
and how God by his almighty Word
filled up the abyss
with that variety and splendor
we daily see around us still.

Let us recall too
how because God first loved us we are.
How, when after a long time
earth was ready
and God with care had prepared a place for man
he brought man forth out of the womb of the earth
and breathed into him his Spirit.
His Spirit.
Like unto himself he brought man forth
in his likeness and in his image.
Like unto the one God he made him
complete within himself, an everlasting value.
Like unto the Trinity he made him
complete like him in a community of love.

God looked at what he had done
and saw that it was very good
and in the cool of the evening
he walked in the garden with man.

For the earth our first mother
and for God our first Father
for day following night
as a sign of his faithfulness
the name of the Lord be praised!

Holy, holy, holy . . .

PREFACE

"Preface!" It is difficult to understand how something so beautiful in word and idea as the preface of the Mass could have gotten so prosaic a name. Just as it is a kind of sadness that something so beautiful as the Mass should have gotten to be called the Mass.

The preface is a hymn of thanks, a paean of praise; we gather up creation in a prayer to the Father.

With the preface we are crossing the threshold of the preliminaries into the great hall of the feast. We have warmed ourselves at the fire; we have made friends with everybody; our hearts are in a generous spirit. We are in our Father's house and he has talked to us. We are in a mood to celebrate.

God is the Father who has surrounded us with all good things. All of creation is a sign of his love, the hymn of his handiwork. His feast is a marriage feast, between lover and beloved.

We are his people and he is our God. Because he loved us we are; because he loves us we continue to be.

The priest voices our praise and thanksgiving. When he has finished we acclaim God: HOLY! HOLY!! HOLY!!! . . .

11. Christ Is Alive

(From the Liturgy of the Word for EASTER SUNDAY) **A B C**

READING I   Acts 10:34, 37-43

A reading from the Acts of the Apostles
We have eaten and drunk with him after his resurrection from the dead.

Peter addressed the people in these words: "I take it you know what has been reported all over Judea about Jesus of Nazareth, beginning in Galilee with the baptism John preached; of the way God anointed him with the Holy Spirit and power. He went about doing good works and healing all who were in the grip of the devil, and God was with him. We are witnesses to all that he did in the land of the Jews and in Jerusalem. They killed him finally, 'hanging him on a tree,' only to have God raise him up on the third day and grant that he be seen, not by all, but only by such witnesses as had been chosen beforehand by God—by us who ate and drank with him after he rose from the dead. He commissioned us to preach to the people and to bear witness that he is the one set apart by God as judge of the living and the dead. To him all the prophets testify, saying that everyone who believes in him has forgiveness of sins through his name."

This is the Word of the Lord.

Responsorial Psalm   Ps 118:1-2, 16-17, 22-23

R.   *(24) This is the day the Lord has made; let us rejoice and be glad.*

Give thanks to the Lord, for he is good,
    for his mercy endures forever.
Let the house of Israel say,
    "His mercy endures forever."

R.   *This is the day the Lord has made; let us rejoice and be glad.*

"The right hand of the Lord has struck with power;
    the right hand of the Lord is exalted.
I shall not die, but live,
    and declare the works of the Lord.

R.   *This is the day the Lord has made; let us rejoice and be glad.*

The stone which the builders rejected
    has become the cornerstone.
By the Lord has this been done;
    It is wonderful in our eyes.

R.   *This is the day the Lord has made; let us rejoice and be glad.*

READING II   Col 3:1-4

A reading from the letter of Paul to the Colossians
Look for the things that are in heaven, where Christ is.

Since you have been raised up in company with
Christ, set your heart on what pertains to higher
realms where Christ is seated at God's right hand.
Be intent on things above rather than on things
of earth. After all, you have died! Your life is
hidden now with Christ in God. When Christ our
life appears, then you shall appear with him in
glory.

> This is the Word of the Lord.

SEQUENCE (Prose text)

To the Paschal Victim let Christians offer a sacrifice of praise.

The Lamb redeemed the sheep. Christ, sinless,
reconciled sinners to the Father.

Death and life were locked together in a unique
struggle. Life's captain died; now he reigns, never
more to die.

Tell us, Mary, "What did you see on the way?"

"I saw the tomb of the now living Christ. I saw
the glory of Christ, now risen.

"I saw angels who gave witness; the cloths too
which once had covered head and limbs.

"Christ my hope has arisen. He will go before
his own into Galilee."

We know that Christ has indeed risen from the
dead. Do you, conqueror and king, have mercy
on us. Amen. Alleluia.

GOSPEL   Jn 20:1-9

R.   *Alleluia.* Christ has become our paschal
            sacrifice;
        let us feast with joy in the Lord.

R.   *Alleluia.*

✠ *A reading from the holy gospel according to
                John*
The teaching of scripture is that he must rise from the dead.

Early in the morning on the first day of the week,
while it was still dark, Mary Magdalene came to
the tomb. She saw that the stone had been moved
away, so she ran off to Simon Peter and the other
disciple (the one Jesus loved) and told them,
"The Lord has been taken from the tomb! We
don't know where they have put him!" At that,
Peter and the other disciple started out on their
way toward the tomb. They were running side by
side, but then the other disciple outran Peter and
reached the tomb first. He did not enter but bent
down to peer in, and saw the wrappings lying on
the ground. Presently, Simon Peter came along
behind him and entered the tomb. He observed
the wrappings on the ground and saw the piece
of cloth which had covered the head not lying
with the wrappings, but rolled up in a place by
itself. Then the disciple who had arrived first at
the tomb went in. He saw and believed. (Remember, as yet they did not understand the Scripture
that Jesus had to rise from the dead.)

> This is the gospel of the Lord.

12. Thanks for God's Mighty Deeds

The priest, with hands extended, says:

Father, we acknowledge your greatness:
all your actions show your wisdom and love.
You formed man in your own likeness
and set him over the whole world
to serve you, his creator,
and to rule over all creatures.
Even when he disobeyed you and lost your
    friendship
you did not abandon him to the power of death,
but helped all men to seek and find you.
Again and again you offered a covenant to man,
and through the prophets taught him to hope for
    salvation.
Father, you so loved the world
that in the fullness of time you sent your only
    Son to be our Savior.
He was conceived through the power of the
    Holy Spirit, and born of the Virgin Mary,
a man like us in all things but sin.
To the poor he proclaimed the good news of
    salvation,
to prisoners, freedom,
and to those in sorrow, joy.
In fulfillment of your will
he gave himself up to death;
but by rising from the dead,
he destroyed death and restored life.
And that we might live no longer for ourselves
    but for him,
he sent the Holy Spirit from you, Father,
as his first gift to those who believe,
to complete his work on earth
and bring us the fullness of grace.

GOD'S MIGHTY DEEDS

Having made man
he loved him with an everlasting love
as only God could.
Having made man
he never forgot him again
not even one of him.
The walking he did with man in the garden
was an everlasting walking by his side
an enduring presence that grew more intimate
as man grew ever more human and more faithful.

From the days of Abraham
when the Lord first appeared to him
and made a covenant with him
and later on dined with him
under the tree before his tent
God moved ever closer to man.
Hand in hand they walked together now
while Abraham grew into a family
and his family into a multitude
and after God had brought the multitude
with signs and wonders out of Egypt
into a people he called his own.
Great things he did for his people
down through the years
and great things he did for us
who followed after in the footsteps
of patriarchs, prophets and kings.

But not content with his being our God
and our being his people
he unfurled his plan fully
when the almighty Word, his Son
leapt down from heaven
to become one of us, a man.
In him God's love for us found final focus.
In him the final age of the world
is come upon us.
In Jesus, our eldest brother,
man has become a son of God.
No more just walking in the garden together
no more just walking hand in hand
in Jesus we are God's sons.
With Jesus we are members of
the one royal household in all the world.
From now on we are in his kingdom
And the kingdom of God is within us.

"IT IS RIGHT..."

The scene is the "upper room" in Jerusalem.

Jesus begins the passover meal with a psalm of praise and thanks to the Father. The youngest member of the group—that would be John—repeats the traditional question which the Jewish boy asks his father: "What is different about this night?" Then Jesus slowly recites the "mighty deeds" of Yahweh who guided his people out of Egypt into the Promised Land . . . from a land of darkness, slavery and ignorance into a new life of freedom, united under one Lord.

As the meal progresses, they look upon—and partake—of the Passover Lamb, a symbol, as they would later realize, of Jesus himself.

The scene is impressive no matter how many times it is recalled.

Two thousand years later, Christians gather at the Eucharist . . . the "Eucharist" which means thanksgiving, a joyful recalling of what God has done for us and *is doing* in us:

"Father, all-powerful and ever-living God, we do well always and everywhere to give you thanks through Jesus Christ our Lord. Through his cross and resurrection he freed us from sin and death and called us to the glory that has made us a chosen race, a royal priesthood, a holy nation, a people set apart. Everywhere we proclaim your mighty works for you have called us out of darkness into your own wonderful light."

So it is particularly appropriate—"it is right"—to give thanks and praise especially at Mass, our passover, our Eucharist, when we remember what God is doing in us.

12. Christ Appears to the Apostles

*(From the Liturgy of the Word for the
SECOND SUNDAY OF EASTER)*

A

READING I Acts 2:42-47

A reading from the Acts of the Apostles
The faithful lived together and owned everything
in common.

The brethren devoted themselves to the apostles' instruction and the communal life, to the breaking of bread and the prayers. A reverent fear overtook them all, for many wonders and signs were performed by the apostles. Those who believed shared all things in common; they would sell their property and goods, dividing everything on the basis of each one's need. They went to the temple area together every day, while in their homes they broke bread. With exultant and sincere hearts they took their meals in common, praising God and winning the approval of all the people. Day by day the Lord added to their number those who were being saved.

This is the Word of the Lord.

Responsorial Psalm Ps 118:2-4, 13-15, 22-24

R. *(1) Give thanks to the Lord for he is good,
his love is everlasting.*

Let the house of Israel say,
  "His mercy endures forever."
Let the house of Aaron say,
  "His mercy endures forever."
Let those who fear the Lord say,
  "His mercy endures forever."

R. *Give thanks to the Lord for he is good, his
love is everlasting.*

I was hard pressed and was falling,
  but the Lord helped me.
My strength and my courage is the Lord,
  and he has been my savior.
The joyful shout of victory
  in the tents of the just:

R. *Give thanks to the Lord for he is good, his
love is everlasting.*

The stone which the builders rejected
  has become the cornerstone.
By the Lord has this been done;
  it is wonderful in our eyes.
This is the day the Lord has made;
  let us be glad and rejoice in it.

R. *Give thanks to the Lord for he is good, his
love is everlasting.*

READING II

1 Pt 1:3-9

A reading from the first letter of Peter

He has given us a new birth as his sons, by raising
Jesus Christ from the dead.

Praised be the God and Father of our Lord Jesus
   Christ,
he who in his great mercy gave us new birth;
a birth unto hope which draws its life
from the resurrection of Jesus Christ from the
   dead;
a birth to an imperishable inheritance
incapable of fading or defilement,
which is kept in heaven for you
who are guarded with God's power through faith;
a birth to a salvation which stands ready
to be revealed in the last days.

There is cause for rejoicing here. You may for
a time have to suffer the distress of many trials;
but this is so that your faith, which is more precious than the passing splendor of fire-tried gold,
may by its genuineness lead to praise, glory, and
honor when Jesus Christ appears. Although you
have never seen him, you love him, and without
seeing you believe in him, and rejoice with in-
expressible joy touched with glory because you
are achieving faith's goal, your salvation.

This is the Word of the Lord

GOSPEL

Jn 20:19-31

Alleluia   Jn 20:29

R.   *Alleluia.* You believe in me, Thomas, be-
         cause you have seen me;
         happy those who have not seen me, but
         still believe!

R.   *Alleluia.*

✛ *A reading from the holy gospel according to
         John*

After eight days Jesus came in and stood among them.

On the evening of that first day of the week, even
though the disciples had locked the doors of the
place where they were for fear of the Jews, Jesus
came and stood before them. "Peace be with
you," he said. When he had said this, he showed
them his hands and his side. At the sight of the
Lord the disciples rejoiced. "Peace be with you,"
he said again.
   "As the Father has sent me,
      so I send you."
Then he breathed on them and said:
   "Receive the Holy Spirit.
   If you forgive men's sins,
      they are forgiven them;
   if you hold them bound,
      they are held bound."

It happened that one of the Twelve, Thomas
(the name means "Twin"), was absent when
Jesus came. The other disciples kept telling him:
"We have seen the Lord!" His answer was, "I'll
never believe it without probing the nail-prints in
his hands, without putting my finger in the nail-
marks and my hand into his side."

A week later, the disciples were once more in
the room, and this time Thomas was with them.
Despite the locked doors, Jesus came and stood
before them. "Peace be with you," he said; then,
to Thomas: "Take your finger and examine my
hands. Put your hand into my side. Do not per-
sist in your unbelief, but believe!" Thomas said
in response, "My Lord and my God!" Jesus then
said to him:
   "You became a believer because you saw me.
   Blest are they who have not seen and have
      believed."

Jesus performed many other signs as well—
signs not recorded here—in the presence of his
disciples. But these have been recorded to help
you believe that Jesus is the Messiah, the Son of
God, so that through this faith you may have life
in his name.

This is the gospel of the Lord.

13. Consecration of Bread and Wine

Father, may this Holy Spirit sanctify these offerings.
Let them become the body ✠ and blood of Jesus Christ our Lord
as we celebrate the great mystery
which he left us as an everlasting covenant.

He always loved those who were his own in the world.
When the time came for him to be glorified by you, his heavenly Father,
he showed the depth of his love.
While they were at supper,
he took bread, said the blessing, broke the bread
and gave it to his disciples, saying:
take this, all of you, and eat it:
this is my body which will be given up for you.

The priest shows the consecrated host to the people, places it on the paten, and genuflects in adoration.

In the same way, he took the cup, filled with wine.
He gave you thanks, and giving the cup to his disciples, said:
Take this, all of you, and drink from it:
this is the cup of my blood,
the blood of the new and everlasting covenant.
It will be shed for you and for all men
so that sins may be forgiven.
Do this in memory of me.

The priest shows the chalice to the people, places it on the corporal, and genuflects in adoration.

CONSECRATION

So that he might become the first
of many, many brothers
Jesus sealed with his blood
our brotherhood with him
and our sonship with God.
He gave us a sign of this seal
the day before he died
three days before he rose again.
He gave us an enduring sign of this seal
of brotherhood and sonship
in the breaking of the bread
and the drinking of the wine.

"With desire," he said
"have I desired to eat this last meal
with you before I suffer."

Then, as they were eating
he took bread, blessed it, and gave thanks
he broke it and gave it to them, saying:
"This is my body to be given for you.
Do this as a remembrance of me."

He did the same with the cup after
eating the bread
saying as he did so:
"This cup is the new covenant in my blood
which will be shed for you."

UNDER THIS SIGN

This above all is the time to believe. Even when Jesus first promised the Eucharist: to give his flesh to eat and his blood to drink, many of his disciples said: "This is hard saying and who can listen to it?"

"Many of his followers," the scripture relates, "turned back, and walked no more with him."

This happened while he was still alive, physically in the midst of men. Should we expect it any easier to believe today? We still have only the words and the command of Jesus: "This is my body and my blood. . . . Do this in memory of me."

Above all we have to believe what we can't see, and really can't understand either, that under this sign made sacred by Jesus, Jesus is present to us. Above all we have to believe, on Jesus' word alone, that in this sacrament the bread and wine brought up and offered are now the body and blood of Christ. They are ours to receive with faith and thanksgiving. Jesus did not explain to his followers when he was alive, nor does he now. Receiving him under the sign of bread and wine we become one together with him.

The essential thing, as always, is invisible to the eye.

13. Christ Appears to Two Disciples

*(From the Liturgy of the Word for the
THIRD SUNDAY OF EASTER)* **A**

READING I   Acts 2:14, 22-28

A reading from the Acts of the Apostles
It was impossible for him to be held by the power of Hades.

[On the day of Pentecost] Peter stood up with the Eleven, raised his voice, and addressed them: "You who are Jews, indeed all of you staying in Jerusalem! Listen to what I have to say: Men of Israel, listen to me! Jesus the Nazorean was a man whom God sent to you with miracles, wonders and signs as his credentials. These God worked through him in your midst, as you well know. He was delivered up by the set purpose and plan of God; you even used pagans to crucify and kill him. God freed him from death's bitter pangs, however, and raised him up again, for it was impossible that death should keep its hold on him. David says of him:

'I have set the Lord ever before me,
  with him at my right hand I shall not be
    disturbed.
My heart has been glad and my tongue has
    rejoiced,
  my body will live on in hope,
For you will not abandon my soul to the nether
    world,
  nor will you suffer your faithful one to
    undergo corruption.
You have shown me the paths of life;
  you will fill me with joy in your presence.' "

This is the Word of the Lord.

Responsorial Psalm   Ps 16:1-2, 5, 7-8, 9-10, 11

R.   *(11) Lord, you will show us the path of life.*

Keep me, O God, for in you I take refuge;
  I say to the Lord, "My Lord are you."
O Lord, my allotted portion and my cup,
  you it is who hold fast my lot.

R.   *Lord, you will show us the path of life.*

I bless the Lord who counsels me;
  even in the night my heart exhorts me.
I set the Lord ever before me;
  with him at my right hand I shall not be dis-
    turbed.

R.   *Lord, you will show us the path of life.*

Therefore my heart is glad and my soul rejoices,
  my body, too, abides in confidence;
Because you will not abandon my soul to the
    nether world,
  nor will you suffer your faithful one to undergo
    corruption.

R.   *Lord, you will show us the path of life.*

You will show me the path to life,
  fullness of joys in your presence,
  the delights at your right hand forever.

R.   *Lord, you will show us the path of life.*

READING II   1 Pt 1:17-21

A reading from the first letter of Peter
The ransom that was paid to free you was the blood of
the Lamb, Jesus Christ.

In prayer you call upon a Father who judges each
one justly, on the basis of his actions. Since this
is so, conduct yourselves reverently during your
sojourn in a strange land. Realize that you were
delivered from the futile way of life your fathers
handed on to you, not by any diminishable sum
of silver or gold but by Christ's blood beyond all
price: the blood of a spotless, unblemished lamb
chosen before the world's foundation and revealed for your sake in these last days. It is
through him you are believers in God, the God
who raised him from the dead and gave him
glory. Your faith and hope, then, are centered in
God.

This is the Word of the Lord.

GOSPEL A   Lk 24:13-35

Alleluia   See Lk 24:32

R.   *Alleluia.* Lord Jesus, make your word plain
        to us,
            make our hearts burn with love when you
            speak.

R.   *Alleluia.*

✠ *A reading from the holy gospel according to
    Luke*
They had recognized him at the breaking of the bread.

Two disciples of Jesus that same day were
making their way to a village named Emmaus
seven miles distant from Jerusalem, discussing
as they went all that had happened. In the
course of their lively exchange, Jesus approached
and began to walk along with them. However,
they were restrained from recognizing him. He
said to them, "What are you discussing as you
go your way?" They halted in distress, and
one of them, Cleopas by name, asked him, "Are
you the only resident of Jerusalem who does
not know the things that went on there these
past few days?" He said to them, "What things?"
They said: "All those that had to do with Jesus
of Nazareth, a prophet powerful in word and deed
in the eyes of God and all the people; how our
chief priests and leaders delivered him up to be
condemned to death, and crucified him. We were
hoping that he was the one who would set Israel
free. Besides all this, today, the third day since
these things happened, some women of our group
have just brought us some astonishing news. They
were at the tomb before dawn and failed to find
his body, but returned with the tale that they had

seen a vision of angels who declared he was alive. Some of our number went to the tomb and found it to be just as the women said; but him they did not see."

Then he said to them, "What little sense you have! How slow you are to believe all that the prophets have announced! Did not the Messiah have to undergo all this so as to enter into his glory?" Beginning, then, with Moses and all the prophets, he interpreted for them every passage of Scripture which referred to him. By now they were near the village to which they were going, and he acted as if he were going farther. But they pressed him: "Stay with us. It is nearly evening— the day is practically over." So he went in to stay with them.

When he had seated himself with them to eat, he took bread, pronounced the blessing, then broke the bread and began to distribute it to them. With that their eyes were opened and they recognized him; whereupon he vanished from their sight. They said to one another, "Were not our hearts burning inside us as he talked to us on the road and explained the Scriptures to us?" They got up immediately and returned to Jerusalem, where they found the Eleven and the rest of the company assembled. They were greeted with, "The Lord has been raised! It is true! He has appeared to Simon." Then they recounted what had happened on the road and how they had come to know him in the breaking of bread.

It was written that the Christ would suffer and on the third day rise from the dead.

The disciples recounted what had happened on the road to Emmaus and how they had come to know Jesus in the breaking of bread.

While they were still speaking about all this, he himself stood in their midst [and said to them, "Peace to you"]. In their panic and fright they thought they were seeing a ghost. He said to them, "Why are you disturbed? Why do such ideas cross your mind? Look at my hands and my feet; it is really I. Touch me, and see that a ghost does not have flesh and bones as I do." [As he said this he showed them his hands and feet.] They were still incredulous for sheer joy and wonder, so he said to them, "Have you anything here to eat?" They gave him a piece of cooked fish, which he took and ate in their presence. Then he said to them, "Recall those words I spoke to you when I was still with you: everything written about me in the law of Moses and the prophets and psalms had to be fulfilled." Then he opened their minds to the understanding of the Scriptures.

He said to them: "Thus it is likewise written that the Messiah must suffer and rise from the dead on the third day. In his name, penance for the remission of sins is to be preached to all the nations, beginning at Jerusalem. You are witnesses to this."

This is the gospel of the Lord.

14. The People's Proclamation

Let us proclaim the mystery of faith:

And the people take up the acclamation:

(a) Christ has died,
     Christ is risen,
     Christ will come again.

Other acclamations:

(b) Dying you destroyed our death,
     rising you restored our life.
     Lord Jesus, come in glory.

(c) When we eat this bread and drink this cup,
     we proclaim your death, Lord Jesus,
     until you come in glory.

(d) Lord, by your cross and resurrection
     you have set us free.
     You are the Savior of the world.

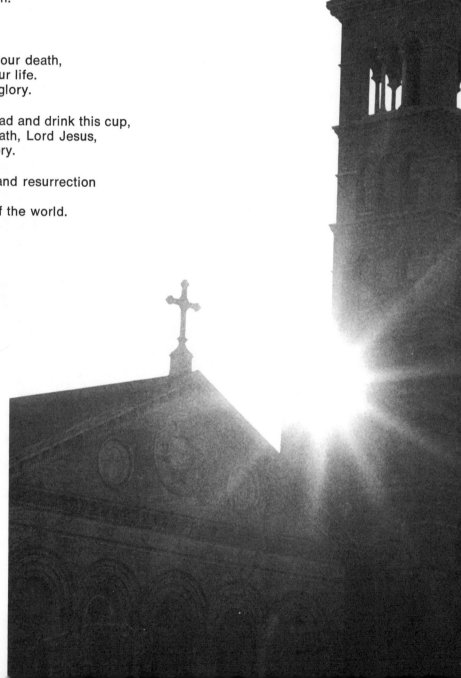

PROCLAMATION

Bread blessed and eaten and
wine blessed and drunk
are the sign of his sacrifice
of his body broken and his blood poured
    out
are the sign of the new relationship of
oneness between God and man and
between man and man.

Let us proclaim now the new mystery
which is ours in the new day of the Lord
in the days of the new relationship with
    God
and with each other:

Jesus our brother
is Christ the Lord
and through his Spirit
we are sons together
of our Father in heaven.

"LET US PROCLAIM . . ."

"Let us proclaim the mystery of faith."

To "proclaim" is to declare publicly, to announce to the world, to shout it out (if we would). Like the partisan at a political rally: Hear! Hear!

Somehow in our devotional life—in our worship—we have forgotten how to proclaim . . . or why.

In our gathering at worship we have just recalled what God has done for us in Christ. We acknowledge his presence among us. We make it a point to dwell lovingly on what he is accomplishing among us. In the face of all the problems in our personal lives and in the world that would say nay, we assert that Christ indeed lives, risen, among us.

There is a psychology about repeating out loud, publicly, what you believe in. If you repeat it often enough, and firmly enough, you begin to grow in conviction. "Tell me what you believe in, what you hope for, and I'll tell you what you are." We are children of God and brothers of Jesus.

If there is any goodness in your life, proclaim it. If there is ignorance, or laxity, or indifference, believe that it can be overcome in Christ: "Dying you destroyed our death, rising you restored our life." Christ's living presence among us here at Mass gives more than human meaning to our striving and to the love and support we show one another.

Our personal restoration to life, and the renewal of the world, obviously, is not automatically accomplished. If you want it to happen at Mass, you have to begin it in your own life. There is no shortcut to life with the risen Christ.

Yet, as we proclaim that Christ has died, is risen, and will come again, we impress it on our consciousness. We become ever more aware each time of his saving power in our lives.

89

14. Christic Appears the Third Time

*(From the Liturgy of the Word for the
THIRD SUNDAY OF EASTER)* **C**

READING I   Acts 5:27-32, 40-41

A reading from the Acts of the Apostles
We are witnesses to all this, we and the Holy Spirit whom
God has given to those who obey him.

The high priest began the interrogation of the apostles in this way: "We gave you strict orders not to teach about that name, yet you have filled Jerusalem with your teaching and are determined to make us responsible for that man's blood." To this, Peter and the apostles replied: "Better for us to obey God than men! The God of our fathers has raised up Jesus whom you put to death, 'hanging him on a tree.' He whom God has exalted at his right hand as ruler and savior is to bring repentance to Israel and forgiveness of sins. We testify to this. So too does the Holy Spirit, whom God has given to those that obey him." The Sanhedrin ordered the apostles not to speak again about the name of Jesus, and afterward dismissed them. The apostles for their part left the Sanhedrin full of joy that they had been judged worthy of ill-treatment for the sake of the Name.

This is the Word of the Lord.

Responsorial Psalm   Ps 30:2, 4, 5-6, 11-12, 13

R. *(2) I will praise you, Lord, for you have rescued me.*

I will extol you, O Lord, for you drew me clear
and did not let my enemies rejoice over me.
O Lord, you brought me up from the nether world;
you preserved me from among those going down into the pit.

R. *I will praise you, Lord, for you have rescued me.*

Sing praise to the Lord, you his faithful ones,
and give thanks to his holy name.
For his anger lasts but a moment;
a lifetime, his good will.
At nightfall, weeping enters in,
but with the dawn, rejoicing.

R. *I will praise you, Lord, for you have rescued me.*

Hear, O Lord, and have pity on me;
O Lord, be my helper.
You changed my mourning into dancing;
O Lord, my God, forever will I give you thanks.

R. *I will praise you, Lord, for you have rescued me.*

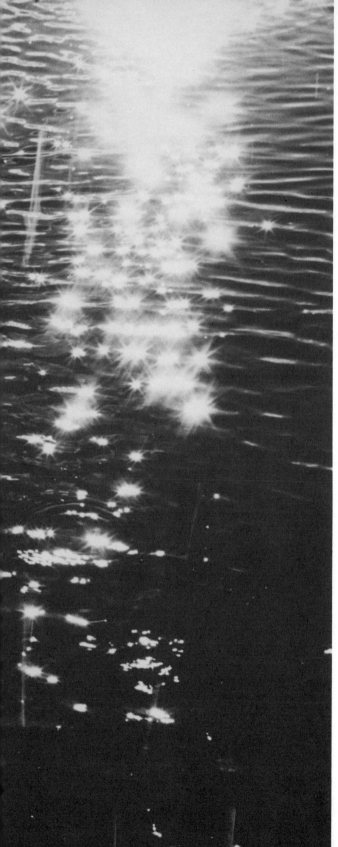

READING II

A reading from the book of Revelation

The Lamb that was sacrificed is worthy to be given power,
wealth, glory, and blessing.

I, John, had a vision, and I heard the voices of
many angels who surrounded the throne and the
living creatures and the elders. They were countless in number, thousands and tens of thousands,
and they all cried out:

"Worthy is the Lamb that was slain
> to receive power and riches, wisdom and
> strength,
> honor and glory and praise!"

Then I heard the voices of every creature in
heaven and on earth and under the earth and
in the sea; everything in the universe cried aloud:

"To the One seated on the throne, and to the
Lamb,
be praise and honor, glory and might,
forever and ever!"

The four living creatures answered, "Amen,"
and the elders fell down and worshiped.

This is the Word of the Lord.

Alleluia   See Lk 24:32

R.   *Alleluia.* Lord Jesus, make your word plain to us,

          make our hearts burn with love when you speak.

R.   *Alleluia.*

✛ *A reading from the holy gospel according to John*

Jesus stepped forward, took the bread and gave it to them, and did the same with the fish.

At the Sea of Tiberias Jesus showed himself to the disciples [once again]. This is how the appearance took place. Assembled were Simon Peter, Thomas ("the Twin"), Nathanael (from Cana in Galilee), Zebedee's sons, and two other disciples. Simon Peter said to them, "I'm going out to fish." "We'll join you," they replied, and went off to get into their boat. All through the night they caught nothing. Just after daybreak Jesus was standing on the shore, though none of the disciples knew it was Jesus. He said to them, "Children, have you caught anything to eat?" "Not a thing," they answered. "Cast your net off to the starboard side," he suggested, "and you will find something." So they made a cast, and took so many fish they could not haul the net in. Then the disciple Jesus loved cried out to Peter, "It is the Lord!" On hearing it was the Lord, Simon Peter threw on some clothes—he was stripped—and jumped into the water.

Meanwhile the other disciples came in the boat, towing the net full of fish. Actually they were not far from land—no more than a hundred yards.

When they landed, they saw a charcoal fire there with a fish laid on it and some bread. "Bring

some of the fish you just caught," Jesus told them. Simon Peter went aboard and hauled ashore the net loaded with sizable fish—one hundred fifty-three of them! In spite of the great number, the net was not torn.

"Come and eat your meal," Jesus told them. Not one of the disciples presumed to inquire "Who are you?" for they knew it was the Lord. Jesus came over, took the bread and gave it to them, and did the same with the fish. This marked the third time that Jesus appeared to the disciples after being raised from the dead.

When they had eaten their meal, Jesus said to Simon Peter, "Simon, son of John, do you love me more than these?" "Yes, Lord," Peter said, "you know that I love you." At which Jesus said, "Feed my lambs."

A second time he put his question, "Simon, son of John, do you love me?" "Yes, Lord," Peter said, "you know that I love you." Jesus replied, "Tend my sheep."

A third time Jesus asked him, "Simon, son of John, do you love me?" Peter was hurt because he had asked a third time, "Do you love me?" So he said to him: "Lord, you know everything. You know well that I love you." Jesus told him, "Feed my sheep.

"I tell you solemnly:
as a young man
you fastened your belt
and went about as you pleased;
but when you are older
you will stretch out your hands,
and another will tie you fast
and carry you off against your will."

(What he said indicated the sort of death by which Peter was to glorify God.) When Jesus had finished speaking he said to him, "Follow me."

This is the gospel of the Lord.

15. The Memorial Prayer

Father, we now celebrate this memorial of our redemption.

We recall Christ's death, his descent among the dead, his resurrection, and his ascension to your right hand; and, looking forward to his coming in glory, we offer you his body and blood,

the acceptable sacrifice which brings salvation to the whole world.

Lord, look upon this sacrifice which you have given to your Church;

and by your Holy Spirit, gather all who share this bread and wine

into the one body of Christ, a living sacrifice of praise.

MEMORIAL

Let us remember this man now
this Jesus our eldest brother
in whom the Father was well pleased
on whom the Spirit descended at his baptism
this Jesus who is the first among us
who freed us from our sins
this Jesus firstborn of all creation
firstfruits of those who have fallen asleep
the first to rise from the dead
so that in him all will come to life again
this Jesus who is Christ the Lord
with whom we are sons of God
let us remember him now and never forget him
neither today, nor tomorrow, nor forever.

So that we might remember him truly
and be the more like him
so that we might recall
all that he was and is
all that he said and did
and fashion ourselves according to him
so that he might teach us all things
necessary down through the ages
so that he might be present within us
and among us
he promised to us the Spirit.
So that we might know him intimately
and each man know him personally
he promised to send his Spirit
upon all who asked him.

The apostles were the first
upon whom he sent his Spirit
and the Spirit transformed them into new men
alive with the new life of Christ.
They worked wonders in his name.
They spoke the good news of Jesus
to all who would listen
and those on whom they laid their hands
in turn received the Spirit.

So has it been down through the ages
those upon whom Jesus sends the Spirit
know him intimately and are transformed
and even while proclaiming the wonders of God
they work wonders themselves in the name of Jesus
the Spirit coming again and again
upon all who asked to be baptized.

THE MASS IS A MEMORIAL

The Mass is a memorial, not a simple remembering. Calvary and the Last Supper are not simply recalled to mind, but actually made present sacramentally.

When our forefathers in the faith recalled at Passover how God led them out of the slavery of Egypt into the desert to make a covenant with them on Mount Sinai, they were not simply remembering their deliverance. They knew it to be a renewal, a re-experiencing of God's great deeds in their lives, and a looking forward to the fulfillment of God's covenant in the Promised Land.

So it is at Mass. In "this memorial of our redemption," we recall Jesus' death, resurrection, ascension, and sending of the Holy Spirit, but we do not simply remember these saving events. Under the sacred signs, Jesus' sacrifice is actually renewed, our covenant is re-experienced, and we look forward to the fulfillment when Christ comes again in glory.

Calvary and the Last Supper continue to be made present at the eucharistic assembly. We look to the past to experience it in the present and to anticipate its fullness in the future.

"Every time, then, you eat this bread and drink this cup, you proclaim the death of the Lord until he comes!"

15. Jesus Leaves

(From the Liturgy of the Word for the ASCENSION) **A B C**

READING I
Acts 1:1-11

The beginning of the Acts of the Apostles
Why are you standing here looking into the sky?
Jesus has been taken into heaven.

In my first account, Theophilus, I dealt with all that Jesus did and taught until the day he was taken up to heaven, having first instructed the apostles he had chosen through the Holy Spirit. In the time after his suffering he showed them in many convincing ways that he was alive, appearing to them over the course of forty days and speaking to them about the reign of God. On one occasion when he met with them, he told them not to leave Jerusalem: "Wait, rather, for the fulfillment of my Father's promise, of which you have heard me speak. John baptized with water, but within a few days you will be baptized with the Holy Spirit."

While they were with him they asked, "Lord, are you going to restore the rule to Israel now?" His answer was: "The exact time it is not yours to know. The Father has reserved that to himself. You will receive power when the Holy Spirit comes down on you; then you are to be my witnesses in Jerusalem, throughout Judea and Samaria, yes, even to the ends of the earth." No sooner had he said this than he was lifted up before their eyes in a cloud which took him from their sight.

They were still gazing up into the heavens when two men dressed in white stood beside them. "Men of Galilee," they said, "why do you stand here looking up at the skies? This Jesus who has been taken from you will return, just as you saw him go up into the heavens."

This is the Word of the Lord.

Responsorial Psalm
Ps 47:2-3, 6-7, 8-9

R. (6) God mounts his throne to shouts of joy; a blare of trumpets for the Lord.

All you peoples, clap your hands,
  shout to God with cries of gladness,
For the Lord, the Most High, the awesome,
  is the great king over all the earth.

R. God mounts his throne to shouts of joy; a blare of trumpets for the Lord.

God mounts his throne amid shouts of joy;
  the Lord, amid trumpet blasts.
Sing praise to God, sing praise;
  sing praise to our king, sing praise.

R. God mounts his throne to shouts of joy; a blare of trumpets for the Lord.

For king of all the earth is God;
  sing hymns of praise.
God reigns over the nations,
  God sits upon his holy throne.

R. God mounts his throne to shouts of joy; a blare of trumpets for the Lord.

READING II
Eph 1:17-23

A reading from the letter of Paul to the Ephesians
He made Jesus to sit at his right hand in heaven.

May the God of our Lord Jesus Christ, the Father of glory, grant you a spirit of wisdom and insight to know him clearly. May he enlighten your innermost vision that you may know the great hope to which he has called you, the wealth of his glorious heritage to be distributed among the members of the church, and the immeasurable scope of his power in us who believe. It is like the strength he showed in raising Christ from the dead and seating him at his right hand in heaven, high above every principality, power, virtue and domination, and every name that can be given in this age or the age to come.

He has put all things under Christ's feet and has made him thus exalted, head of the church, which is his body: the fullness of him who fills the universe in all its parts.

This is the Word of the Lord.

GOSPEL A   Mt 28:16-20

Alleluia   Mt 28:19-20

R.   *Alleluia.* Go and teach all people my gospel.
            I am with you always, until the end of
            the world.
R.   *Alleluia.*

✠ *The conclusion of the holy gospel according to Matthew*
All authority in heaven and on earth has been given to me.

The eleven disciples made their way to Galilee, to the mountain to which Jesus had summoned them. At the sight of him, those who had entertained doubts fell down in homage. Jesus came forward and addressed them in these words:
    "Full authority has been given to me
        both in heaven and on earth;
        go, therefore, and make disciples of all the
            nations.
    Baptize them in the name
        'of the Father,
        and of the Son,
        and of the Holy Spirit.'
    Teach them to carry out everything I have
        commanded you.
    And know that I am with you always,
        until the end of the world!"

GOSPEL B   Mk 16:15-20

✠ *The conclusion of the holy gospel according to Mark*
The Lord Jesus was taken up into heaven and is seated at the right hand of God.

[Jesus appeared to the Eleven and] said to them: "Go into the whole world and proclaim the good news to all creation. The man who believes in it and accepts baptism will be saved; the man who refuses to believe in it will be condemned. Signs like these will accompany those who have professed their faith: they will use my name to expel demons, they will speak entirely new languages, they will be able to handle serpents, they will be able to drink deadly poison without harm, and the sick upon whom they lay their hands will recover." Then, after speaking to them, the Lord Jesus was taken up into heaven and took his seat at God's right hand. The Eleven went forth and preached everywhere. The Lord continued to work with them throughout and confirm the message through the signs which accompanied them.

GOSPEL C   Lk 24:46-53

✠ *The conclusion of the holy gospel according to Luke*
He blessed them, withdrew from them, and was carried up to heaven.

Jesus said to the Eleven: "Thus it is written that the Messiah must suffer and rise from the dead on the third day. In his name, penance for the remission of sins is to be preached to the nations, beginning at Jerusalem. You are witnesses of all this. See, I send down upon you the promise of my Father. Remain here in the city until you are clothed with power from on high."

He then led them out near Bethany, and with hands upraised, blessed them. As he blessed, he left them, and was taken up to heaven. They fell down to do him reverence, then returned to Jerusalem filled with joy. There they were to be found in the temple constantly, speaking the praises of God.

This is the gospel of the Lord.

16. Prayer for the Living and the Dead

Lord, remember those for whom we offer this
  sacrifice,
especially N. our Pope,
N. our bishop, and bishops and clergy everywhere.
Remember those who take part in this offering,
those here present and all your people,
and all who seek you with a sincere heart.
Remember those who have died in the peace of
  Christ
and all the dead whose faith is known to you
  alone.
Father, in your mercy grant also to us, your
  children,
to enter into our heavenly inheritance
in the company of the Virgin Mary, the Mother
  of God,
and your apostles and saints.
Then, in your kingdom, freed from the corrup-
  tion of sin and death,
we shall sing your glory with every creature
  through Christ our Lord,

He joins his hands:

through whom you give us everything that is
  good.

COMMEMORATION

We pray, therefore:
Send anew upon the world today
upon the high and the low in all places
send anew upon your Church today
upon all of us who claim your name
your Spirit, Lord Jesus.

Touch us as you touched the apostles
with fiery tongues and a burning desire.
Touch us as your Father did of old
the lips of the prophet with a live coal.
Make contact with us
put your finger on us
lay your hands upon us
shine your face on us
transform us
shape us to yourself
renew us in your Spirit
for without you we do nothing.
Without your Spirit
we are paupers before you
and remember you but poorly.
Without your Spirit
we know you only feebly
as out of a book
second hand.

Make yourself real to us, therefore,
by sending your Spirit upon us
so that you will be in us and we in you
so that we may at last proclaim
each of us from the housetops:
"Finally and at long last I live
because Jesus is the Lord
and Christ is alive in me."

Remembering the Christ who lives in us
we who live in him
also recall with hope in our hearts
those who have died.

THE MASS IS A REMEMBRANCE

At the last supper in the close companionship of the upper room after the institution of the Eucharist, Jesus spoke of many things with his apostles. "You are my friends," he said to them, "I have called you friends and told you everything. My Father keep you now. Not only you, but all who will believe in me. That they may all be one, as you, Father in me, and I in you."

There is a tone of intimacy and of love in the long discourse, as Jesus commemorates the time he spent among them.

And now we call to mind, and commemorate, the passion, death and resurrection of our friend Jesus. We call to mind and commemorate the whole happy family of Christ's friends, living and dead: his mother, the apostles, the martyrs down the years, the saints of all time, those trying to be his friends this very day, the entire people of God, the family gathered together before him in church, those we know and those who are in need: the poor, the sick, victims of all kinds; our brothers and sisters who have gone to their rest in the hope of rising again. . . .

We call to mind, we commemorate, for to remember someone is already to make him present among us.

16. Awaiting the Spirit

(From the Liturgy of the Word for the **A B C**
VIGIL OF PENTECOST)

READING I   Jl 3:1-5

A reading from the book of the prophet Joel
I will pour out my spirit on all mankind.

Thus says the Lord:
  I will pour out
    my spirit upon all mankind.
  Your sons and daughters shall prophesy,
    your old men shall dream dreams,
    your young men shall see visions;
  Even upon the servants and the handmaids,
    in those days, I will pour out my spirit.
  And I will work wonders in the heavens and on
      the earth,
    blood, fire, and columns of smoke;
  The sun will be turned to darkness,
    and the moon to blood,
  At the coming of the Day of the Lord,
    the great and terrible day.
  Then everyone shall be rescued
    who calls on the name of the Lord;
  For on Mount Zion there shall be a remnant,
    as the Lord has said,
  And in Jerusalem survivors
    whom the Lord shall call.

        This is the Word of the Lord.

Responsorial Psalm
        Ps 104:1-2, 24, 35, 27-28, 29, 30

R. *(30) Lord, send out your Spirit, and renew
      the face of the earth.*

Bless the Lord, O my soul!
  O Lord, my God, you are great indeed!
You are clothed with majesty and glory,
  robed in light as with a cloak.

R. *Lord, send out your Spirit, and renew the
      face of the earth.*

How manifold are your works, O Lord!
  In wisdom you have wrought them all—
  the earth is full of your creatures;
  Bless the Lord, O my soul! Alleluia.

R. *Lord, send out your Spirit, and renew the
      face of the earth.*

Creatures all look to you
  to give them food in due time.
When you give it to them, they gather it;
  when you open your hand, they are filled with
      good things.

R. *Lord, send out your Spirit, and renew the
      face of the earth.*

If you take away their breath, they perish
  and return to their dust.
When you send forth your spirit, they are created,
  and you renew the face of the earth.

R. *Lord, send out your Spirit, and renew the
      face of the earth.*

READING II   Rom 8:22-27

A reading from the letter of Paul to the Romans
The Spirit himself pleads for us in a way that could never
be put into words.

We know that all creation groans and is in agony
even until now. Not only that, but we ourselves,
although we have the Spirit as first fruits, groan
inwardly while we await the redemption of our
bodies. In hope we were saved. But hope is not
hope if it its object is seen; how is it possible for
one to hope for what he sees? And hoping for
what we cannot see means awaiting it with patient
endurance.

The Spirit too helps us in our weakness, for
we do not know how to pray as we ought; but the
Spirit himself makes intercession for us with
groanings which cannot be expressed in speech.
He who searches hearts knows what the Spirit
means, for the Spirit intercedes for the saints as
God himself wills.

This is the Word of the Lord.

GOSPEL   Jn 7:37-39

Alleluia

R.   *Alleluia.* Come, Holy Spirit, fill the hearts of
            your faithful;
         and kindle in them the fire of your love.
R.   *Alleluia.*

✠ *A reading from the holy gospel according to
                    John*
From his breast shall flow fountains of living waters.

On the last and greatest day of the festival, Jesus
stood up and cried out:
    "If anyone thirsts, let him come to me;
    Let him drink who believes in me.
    Scripture has it:
        'From within him rivers of living water shall
            flow.' "
(Here he was referring to the Spirit, whom those
that came to believe in him were to receive. There
was, of course, no Spirit as yet, since Jesus had
not yet been glorified.)

This is the gospel of the Lord.

17. Doxology and the Great Amen

The priest takes the chalice and the paten with the host and, lifting them up, says:

Through him,

with him,

in him,

in the unity of the Holy Spirit,

all glory and honor is yours,

almighty Father,

for ever and ever.

The people respond:

Amen.

17. Doxology

Through this Jesus
who is the Christ
who is the Lord
and through the Spirit
he has sent
God our Father be praised
today and every day
and beyond all days forever.

Amen.

(end of eucharistic prayer)

THE MASS IS A DIALOGUE

The Mass is a conversation with God. We talk to him and he talks to us, as during the Penitential Rite and the Liturgy of the Word. The Mass is also a dialogue between priest and people.

The dialogue between priest and people is a real one; it should really be heard. That is why some of the people's parts are called "acclamations."

There are three of them during the eucharistic prayer, and we ought to acclaim in no uncertain terms our approval of what the priest is doing and saying.

The first of these acclamations is the "holy, holy, holy" after the hymn of praise. The second is the proclamation after the consecration. It has several forms. The third is the great "Amen" at the end of the eucharistic prayer.

Do you approve of the high and holy things happening before your very eyes? If you do not, what are you doing here? If you do, then let yourself be heard.

After the priest consecrates he "shows" the bread to the people, and he "shows" the cup to the people, but here at the end of the eucharistic prayer he "lifts them up" to the Lord. "If I be lifted up, I shall draw all things to myself."

It is a solemn and satisfying moment. The great "Amen" is a ratifying event.

THE GREAT "AMEN"

The great St. Teresa once remarked that if people really knew what they were signing themselves up for when they prayed, they wouldn't do it lightly.

"Let it be!" we say. "Amen" . . . "yes" . . . we agree completely with God's plan. We open ourselves to the full potential of God's word in us.

Ours cannot be a casual response. We are committed to more than we can imagine.

All things were made through Christ, St. John tells us. St. Paul follows with the strange statement that if any man is in Christ, he is a "new creation." "The old creation where men lived only for themselves has gone, and now the new one is here. It is all God's work. It was God who reconciled us to himself through Christ and gave us the work of handing on this reconciliation."

This work is demanding. It is no less than the making of "a new heaven and a new earth." "Behold, I make all things new," says God: where men live no longer for themselves.

As in baptism, in each Mass we are again plunged into Christ's death and resurrection: death to all that resists God and his plan to be realized in us, death to all that is opposed to the new community that he came to found, death to all that is not love.

And resurrection to all that is risen life: love, joy, peace, patience—the fruits of the Spirit who is given to us.

At Mass we pledge ourselves to no less than the making of a new world. But we would not be able to do anything without Christ.

Christ gives us himself at Mass.

17. The Spirit Comes

(From the Liturgy of the Word for PENTECOST SUNDAY) **A B C**

READING I
Acts 2:1-11

A reading from the Acts of the Apostles
They were all filled with the Holy Spirit, and began to speak in different languages.

When the day of Pentecost came it found the brethren gathered in one place. Suddenly from up in the sky there came a noise like a strong, driving wind which was heard all through the house where they were seated. Tongues as of fire appeared which parted and came to rest on each of them. All were filled with the Holy Spirit. They began to express themselves in foreign tongues and make bold proclamation as the Spirit prompted them.

Staying in Jerusalem at the time were devout Jews of every nation under heaven. These heard the sound, and assembled in a large crowd. They were much confused because each one heard these men speaking his own language. The whole occurrence astonished them. They asked in utter amazement, "Are not all of these men who are speaking Galileans? How is it that each of us hears them in his native tongue? We are Parthians, Medes, and Elamites. We live in Mesopotamia, Judea and Cappadocia, Pontus, the province of Asia, Phrygia and Pamphylia, Egypt, and the regions of Libya around Cyrene. There are even visitors from Rome—all Jews, or those who have come over to Judaism; Cretans and Arabs too. Yet each of us hears them speaking in his own tongue about the marvels God has accomplished."

This is the Word of the Lord.

Responsorial Psalm   Ps 104:1, 24, 29-30, 31, 34

R. (30) Lord, send out your Spirit, and renew the face of the earth.

Bless the Lord, O my soul!
   O Lord, my God, you are great indeed!
How manifold are your works, O Lord!
   the earth is full of your creatures.

R. Lord, send out your Spirit, and renew the face of the earth.

If you take away their breath, they perish and
   return to their dust.
When you send forth your spirit, they are created,
   and you renew the face of the earth.

R. Lord, send out your Spirit, and renew the face of the earth.

May the glory of the Lord endure forever;
   may the Lord be glad in his works!
Pleasing to him be my theme;
   I will be glad in the Lord.

R. Lord, send out your Spirit, and renew the face of the earth.

READING II
1 Cor 12:3-7, 12-13

A reading from the first letter of Paul to the Corinthians
In one Spirit we were all baptized, making one body.

No one can say: "Jesus is Lord," except in the Holy Spirit.

There are different gifts but the same Spirit; there are different ministries but the same Lord; there are different works but the same God who accomplishes all of them in every one. To each person the manifestation of the Spirit is given for the common good.

The body is one and has many members, but all the members, many though they are, are one body; and so it is with Christ. It was in one Spirit that all of us, whether Jew or Greek, slave or free, were baptized into one body. All of us have been given to drink of the one Spirit.

This is the Word of the Lord.

SEQUENCE (Prose text)

Come, Holy Spirit, and from heaven direct on man the rays of your light. Come, Father of the poor; come, giver of God's gifts; come, light of men's hearts.

Kindly Paraclete, in your gracious visits to man's soul you bring relief and consolation. If it is weary with toil, you bring it ease; in the heat of temptation, your grace cools it; if sorrowful, your words console it.

Light most blessed, shine on the hearts of your faithful—even into their darkest corners; for without your aid man can do nothing good, and everything is sinful.

Wash clean the sinful soul, rain down your grace on the parched soul and heal the injured soul. Soften the hard heart, cherish and warm the ice-cold heart, and give direction to the wayward.

Give your seven holy gifts to your faithful, for their trust is in you. Give them reward for their virtuous acts; give them a death that ensures salvation; give them unending bliss. Amen. Alleluia.

GOSPEL   Jn 20:19-23

Alleluia

R.   *Alleluia.* Come, Holy Spirit, fill the hearts of
            your faithful;
        and kindle in them the fire of your love.
R.   *Alleluia.*

✠ *A reading from the holy gospel according to John*
As the Father sent me, so I send you:
Receive the Holy Spirit.

On the evening of that first day of the week, even though the disciples had locked the doors of the place where they were for fear of the Jews, Jesus came and stood before them. "Peace be with you," he said. When he had said this, he showed them his hands and his side. At the sight of the Lord the disciples rejoiced. "Peace be with you," he said again.

"As the Father has sent me,
    so I send you."
Then he breathed on them and said:
"Receive the Holy Spirit.
If you forgive men's sins,
    they are forgiven them;
    if you hold them bound,
    they are held bound."

This is the gospel of the Lord.

PART 4

The Rite of Communion

18. The Our Father

Priest: Let us pray with confidence to the Father
in the words our Savior gave us:

All: Our Father, who art in heaven,
hallowed be thy name:
thy kingdom come;
thy will be done on earth as it is in heaven.
Give us this day our daily bread;
and forgive us our trespasses
as we forgive those who trespass against us;
and lead us not into temptation,
but deliver us from evil.

Priest: Deliver us, Lord, from every evil,
and grant us peace in our day.
In your mercy keep us free from sin
and protect us from all anxiety
as we wait in joyful hope
for the coming of our Savior, Jesus Christ.

People: For the kingdom, the power, and the glory are yours, now and for ever.

PRAY WITH CONFIDENCE

The natural thing for us here is to stress that we pray "in the words our Savior gave us." What could be more acceptable to the Father than the very words of his Son?

But the Church very wisely also counsels us to "pray with confidence" because that is the way the Son prays. It is not only the words we say, but how we say them. The effectiveness of our prayer depends on our faith.

Christ prayed as a son: "Father, I know that you always hear me . . . Father, everything that is yours is mine." Dare we pray that way?

"I tell you solemnly," says Jesus, "if anyone says to this mountain, 'Get up and throw yourself into the sea,' with no hesitation in his heart but believing that what he says will happen, it will be done for him." He continues with an even more startling statement: "I tell you therefore: everything you ask and pray for, believe that you have it already, and it will be yours."

Believe that you have it already!

Father, we know you want us to ask, because your Son said we should. But we know also that you know our wants even before we ask, for the Spirit in us speaks of our needs "with sighs too deep for words."

Father, let us also know, with Jesus your Son, that you indeed always hear us and will us good, for all that you have is ours. What more could you give us than what you already have in your Son Jesus, through whom you give us all good things?

Do we pray that your kingdom come? It is already begun. Our daily bread? Forgiveness? Final salvation? Help us, as you said, to believe we have it already, and it will be ours!

OUR FATHER

Many people do not realize how preoccupied Jesus was with talking about his Father and about revealing his Father to us.

The Father is mentioned over 250 times in the New Testament; 200 times in the gospels alone. Jesus talks about him as "my Father," "your Father," "the Father," "God the Father," and "our Father."

The Father is a New Testament revelation by Jesus. The very few times the "Lord, Father" is mentioned in the Old Testament seems almost an accident.

Jesus alone knew the Father and he talked about him endlessly. He obviously wanted very much that men know his Father and that they learn to love his Father as he did. To know him was to love him: He is all things good, true and beautiful. "If you ask the Father anything in my name he will give it to you."

Jesus himself prayed to the Father often: "I confess to thee, O Father . . ." "Abba, Father . . ." "Father, if you will, remove this chalice . . ." "Father, into your hands . . ."

That is why, if we are going to ask Jesus for a prayer and he is going to give us one, it can only begin in the one way it did: "Our Father . . ." and the prayer is going to talk about our Father and us.

18. This Is My Body

(From the Liturgy of the Word for CORPUS CHRISTI)

A

READING I Dt 8:2-3, 14-16

A reading from the book of Deuteronomy
He gave you food which you and your fathers did not know.

Moses said to the people: "Remember how for forty years now the Lord, your God, has directed all your journeying in the desert, so as to test you by affliction and find out whether or not it was your intention to keep his commandments. He therefore let you be afflicted with hunger, and then fed you with manna, a food unknown to you and your fathers, in order to show you that not by bread alone does man live, but by every word that comes forth from the mouth of the Lord.

"Remember, the Lord, your God, who brought you out of the land of Egypt, that place of slavery; who guided you through the vast and terrible desert with its saraph serpents and scorpions, its parched and waterless ground; who brought forth water for you from the flinty rock and fed you in the desert with manna, a food unknown to your fathers."

This is the Word of the Lord.

Responsorial Psalm Ps 147:12-13, 14-15, 19-20

R. *(12) Praise the Lord, Jerusalem.*

Glorify the Lord, O Jerusalem;
    praise your God, O Zion.
For he has strengthened the bars of your gates;
    he has blessed your children within you.

R. *Praise the Lord, Jerusalem.*

He has granted peace in your borders;
    with the best of wheat he fills you.
He sends forth his command to the earth;
    swiftly runs his word!

R. *Praise the Lord, Jerusalem.*

He has proclaimed his word to Jacob,
    his statutes and his ordinances to Israel.
He has not done thus for any other nation;
    his ordinances he has not made known to them.
        Alleluia.

R. *Praise the Lord, Jerusalem.*

READING II   1 Cor 10:16-17

A reading from the first letter of Paul to the Corinthians

Though we are many, we form a single body because we share this one loaf.

Is not the cup of blessing we bless a sharing in the blood of Christ? And is not the bread we break a sharing in the body of Christ? Because the loaf of bread is one, we, many though we are, are one body for we all partake of the one loaf.

This is the Word of the Lord.

SEQUENCE (Prose Text)

Zion, praise your Savior. Praise your leader and shepherd in hymns and canticles. Praise him as much as you can, for he is beyond all praising and you will never be able to praise him as he merits.

But today a theme worthy of particular praise is put before us—the living and life-giving bread that, without any doubt, was given to the Twelve at table during the holy supper.

Therefore let our praise be full and resounding and our soul's rejoicing full of delight and beauty, for this is the festival day to commemorate the first institution of this table.

At this table of the new King, the new law's new Pasch puts an end to the old Pasch. The new displaces the old, reality the shadow and light the darkness. Christ wanted what he did at the supper to be repeated in his memory.

And so we, in accordance with his holy directions, consecrate bread and wine to be salvation's Victim. Christ's followers know by faith that bread is changed into his flesh and wine into his blood.

Man cannot understand this, cannot perceive it; but a lively faith affirms that the change, which is outside the natural course of things, takes place. Under the different species, which are now signs only and not their own reality, there lie hid wonderful realities. His body is our food, his blood our drink.

And yet Christ remains entire under each species. The communicant receives the complete Christ—uncut, unbroken and undivided. Whether one receives or a thousand, the one receives as much as the thousand. Nor is Christ diminished by being received.

The good and the wicked alike receive him, but with the unlike destiny of life or death. To the wicked it is death, but life to the good. See how different is the result, though each receives the same.

Last of all, if the sacrament is broken, have no doubt. Remember there is as much in a fragment as in an unbroken host. There is no division of the reality, but only a breaking of the sign; nor does the breaking diminish the condition or size of the One hidden under the sign.

Behold, the bread of angels is become the pilgrim's food; truly it is bread for the sons, and is not to be cast to dogs. It was prefigured in type when Isaac was brought as an offering, when a lamb was appointed for the Pasch and when manna was given to the Jews of old.

Jesus, good shepherd and true bread, have mercy on us; feed us and guard us. Grant that we find happiness in the land of the living. You know all things, can do all things, and feed us here on earth. Make us your guests in heaven, co-heirs with you and companions of heaven's citizens. Amen. Alleluia.

GOSPEL B

Alleluia   Jn 6:51-52

R.   *Alleluia*. I am the living bread from heaven,
      says the Lord;
          if anyone eats this bread he will live for-
              ever.

R.   *Alleluia*.

 *A reading from the holy gospel according to
Mark*
This is my body. This is my blood.

On the first day of Unleavened Bread, when it
was customary to sacrifice the paschal lamb, the
disciples said to Jesus, "Where do you wish us to
go to prepare the Passover supper for you?" He
sent two of his disciples with these instructions:
"Go into the city and you will come upon a man
carrying a water jar. Follow him. Whatever house
he enters, say to the owner, 'The Teacher asks,
Where is my guestroom where I may eat the Passover with my disciples?' Then he will show you
an upstairs room, spacious, furnished, and all in
order. That is the place you are to get ready for
us." The disciples went off. When they reached
the city they found it just as he had told them,
and they prepared the Passover supper.

During the meal he took bread, blessed and
broke it, and gave it to them. "Take this," he
said, "this is my body." He likewise took a cup,
gave thanks and passed it to them, and they all
drank from it. He said to them: "This is my
blood, the blood of the covenant, to be poured
out on behalf of many. I solemnly assure you, I
will never again drink of the fruit of the vine
until the day when I drink it new in the reign of
God."

After singing songs of praise they walked out
to the Mount of Olives.

This is the gospel of the Lord.

19. The Sign of Peace

The priest continues:

Priest: Lord Jesus Christ, you said to your apostles:
I leave you peace, my peace I give you.
Look not on our sins, but on the faith of your Church,
and grant us the peace and unity of your kingdom
where you live for ever and ever.

People: Amen.

Priest: The peace of the Lord be with you always.

People: And also with you.

The priest may add:

Priest: Let us offer each other the sign of peace.

The sign of peace is made according to local custom.

SIGN OF PEACE

There is much talk of peace . . . at a time when there has never been more division: between husband/wife, parent/child, liberal/conservative, hawk/dove. Yet Christ came to heal divisions: between God and man, between man and man.

We come to Mass to be reconciled and to be reconcilers . . .

But we should not deceive ourselves. We cannot come to Mass with hates stored up inside and expect a few gestures to disgorge them. Divisions are not healed without anguish, as Christ's sacrifice was not accomplished without the cross.

Christ did not come to bring a false peace: "Do not suppose that I have come to bring peace to the earth: it is not peace I have come to bring, but a sword."

The "sword" of Christ is not a sword of dissension so much as a sword of values, the priority of truth. What Christ is, and what he stands for, causes divisions in our world because everyone is not equally for the truth, and where there is no meeting of hearts in Christ there can be no peace. (But when people meet in Christ, there is peace despite differences.)

There is a further cause of hate and division: We fight against the "dark forces" in man, against "principalities and powers," against Satan himself, the prince of division.

Fortunately, we have a Lord who is stronger than all the forces of evil. "Peace I bequeath to you," he said, "my own peace I give you, a peace the world cannot give. . . . Do not let your hearts be troubled or afraid."

SIGN OF LOVE

It is here in the new Mass by way of an option: ". . . *the priest may add:* Let us show that we are at peace with one another. *All make some appropriate customary sign of peace and love.*"

"We've come a long way," writes Mary Reed Newland. "The other evening at a Lenten Mass—our pastor who is 60 explained what the Mass was supposed to be '. . . a gathering of people who love the Lord and one another, are grateful that he died for us, who come together to enjoy a meal with him—a sacred one—to share their joy and their trials, to pray for strength, give thanks, and go out into the world better able to cope. . . .

" 'We ought to show our joy, smile at each other as we go to the table and return. We ought to feel relaxed and comfortable because we are friends and the Lord is our friend. . . . And it is beyond me to hear Americans who have such a variety of ways to greet each other, say they don't know what to do at the greeting of Peace. Do whatever is most comfortable and natural, but do greet one another with love in the name of the Lord . . . and if there is anyone present who cannot bring himself to greet some other one in the congregation, it would be better if such a person went home and did not come the next time.'

"I don't know about the rest of them, but the Mass had arrived for me. I quietly bawled. And because I am a kissing kind of person, at the Peace I kissed Flora Beaulieu, and Agnes Foley, and Grandma Billodeau, and the love between us all but made music. Afterward I went into the sacristy and hugged the pastor."

19. Where Shall We Buy Bread...?

(From the Liturgy of the Word for the SEVENTEENTH SUNDAY OF THE YEAR) **B**

READING I 2 Kgs 4:42-44

A reading from the second book of Kings
They will eat, and have some left over.

A man came from Baal-shalishah bringing to Elisha, the man of God, twenty barley loaves made from the firstfruits, and fresh grain in the ear. "Give it to the people to eat," Elisha said. But his servant objected, "How can I set this before a hundred men?" "Give it to the people to eat," Elisha insisted. "For thus says the Lord, 'They shall eat and there shall be some left over.' " And when they had eaten, there was some left over, as the Lord had said.

This is the Word of the Lord.

Responsorial Psalm Ps 145:10-11, 15-16, 17-18

R. (16) The hand of the Lord feeds us; he answers all our needs.

Let all your works give you thanks, O Lord,
    and let your faithful ones bless you.
Let them discourse of the glory of your kingdom
    and speak of your might.

R. The hand of the Lord feeds us; he answers all our needs.

The eyes of all look hopefully to you,
    and you give them their food in due season;
You open your hand
    and satisfy the desire of every living thing.

R. The hand of the Lord feeds us; he answers all our needs.

The Lord is just in all his ways
    and holy in all his works.
The Lord is near to all who call upon him,
    to all who call upon him in truth.

R. The hand of the Lord feeds us; he answers all our needs.

READING II Eph 4:1-6

A reading from the letter of Paul to the Ephesians
There is one body, one Lord, one faith, one baptism.

I plead with you as a prisoner for the Lord, to live a life worthy of the calling you have received, with perfect humility, meekness, and patience, bearing with one another lovingly. Make every effort to preserve the unity which has the Spirit as its origin and peace as its binding force. There is but one body and one Spirit, just as there is but one hope given all of you by your call. There is one Lord, one faith, one baptism; one God and Father of all, who is over all, and works through all, and is in all.

This is the Word of the Lord.

GOSPEL   Jn 6:1-15

Alleluia   Jn 8:12

R.   *Alleluia.* I am the light of the world, says the
       Lord;
          the man who follows me will have the
             light of life.

R.   *Alleluia.*

✠ *A reading from the holy gospel according to
                    John*
He distributed to those who were seated as much
                as they wanted.

Jesus crossed the Sea of Galilee [to the shore] of
Tiberias; a vast crowd kept following him because
they saw the signs he was performing for the sick.
Jesus then went up the mountain and sat down
there with his disciples. The Jewish feast of Passover was near; when Jesus looked up and caught
sight of a vast crowd coming toward him, he said
to Philip, "Where shall we buy bread for these
people to eat?" (He knew well what he intended
to do but he asked this to test Philip's response.)
Philip replied, "Not even with two hundred days'
wages could we buy loaves enough to give each
of them a mouthful!"

One of Jesus' disciples, Andrew, Simon Peter's
brother, remarked to him, "There is a lad here
who has five barley loaves and a couple of dried
fish, but what good is that for so many?" Jesus
said, "Get the people to recline." Even though
the men numbered about five thousand, there
was plenty of grass for them to find a place on
the ground. Jesus then took the loaves of bread,
gave thanks, and passed them around to those
reclining there; he did the same with the dried
fish, as much as they wanted. When they had had
enough, he told his disciples, "Gather up the
crusts that are left over so that nothing will go to
waste." At this, they gathered twelve baskets full
of pieces left over by those who had been fed with
the five barley loaves.

When the people saw the sign he had performed they began to say, "This is undoubtedly
the Prophet who is to come into the world." At
that Jesus realized that they would come and
carry him off to make him king, so he fled back
to the mountain alone.

This is the gospel of the Lord.

20. The Lamb of God

The priest then breaks the host, places a small piece in the chalice, saying quietly:

Priest: May this mingling of the body and blood of our Lord Jesus Christ bring eternal life to us who receive it.

Then the following is sung or said:

All: Lamb of God, you take away the sins of the world:
  have mercy on us.
Lamb of God, you take away the sins of the world:
  have mercy on us.
Lamb of God, you take away the sins of the world:
  grant us peace.

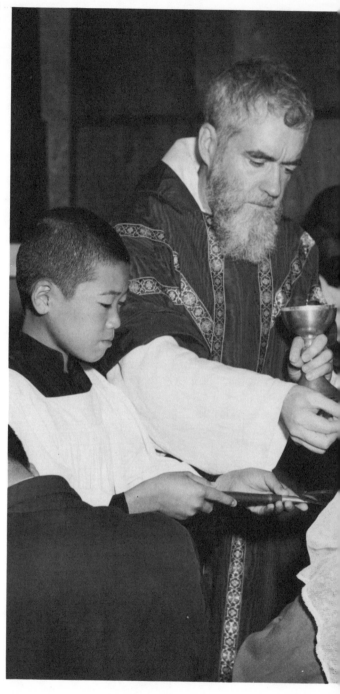

LAMB OF GOD

At Mass we recognize Christ as the Lamb who was slain. We hail him as the one Man on earth who became so deeply involved with our whole guilty world that he became, in Paul's words, sin.

To be a Christian—to be present at Mass—means to be willing also to take on the sins of the world, as Christ did, and to be a savior with him.

The sins of the world! It is a sad discovery for every man as he grows older that life is one long discovery of evil in the world, or so it seems. He discovers there are such disorders as sins of the world which man cannot cope with himself and which carry him along like a torrent, movements of evil which take mankind in, and which except for the Lamb of God would have the upper hand.

Happily, we are not called upon to solve the problem of the world's evil. Christ did not solve the problem of evil, of sin, of guilt. He took it upon himself. To be a Christian means to do likewise.

We begin to be saviors with Christ when we realize that we are somehow involved in the sin, the guilt, of the world. Most of us are willing to recognize our obvious personal sins; we are less willing to admit to consciousness those which are less obvious and which constitute our share in the sins of the world. Many of us rarely come to the realization that our sins extend beyond ourselves and our immediate surroundings. Because of that we can never be saviors.

But there have always been people who were willing to be so: the wife of an alcoholic, the parent of a teenage drug addict, the survivor of a concentration camp who want to help, who patiently wait, who refuse to hate.

"Whenever this strength—we call it forgiveness—is visible, the fatality of evil is broken and the world is justified. Such people are greater than sin. They do not solve the problem of guilt. But, in their lives, they bear it away. They are the people who take away the sins of the world"—(Huub Oosterhuis). They are those who have made themselves one with the Savior.

THE BREAKING OF THE BREAD

It is one of the most delightful stories in scripture how those two disciples on their way to Emmaus were taken in by the stranger and the stranger allowed them to be taken in by him. They were sad because Jesus had been crucified. And the stranger asked them: "Did not the Christ have to suffer?" He expounded the scriptures to them to prove it. When they arrived at Emmaus they invited the stranger in because it was already late by then. At supper they recognized the stranger "in the breaking of the bread," and with that the risen Jesus was gone from them. "Did not our hearts burn within us when he was talking to us?" They did indeed. There is a happy ending to the story of Jesus: He is risen, he is among us.

The bread is broken as Christ was broken for the sins of the world.

The bread is broken while the Lamb of God is asked to take away the sins of the world.

The bread is broken so that we may all share in it.

It is a rich moment at Mass. It is a point of convergence in which memorial, meal, and sacrifice come together and can all be seen at once, when Christ's dying for the sins of the world, our remembering, and our sharing Christ, crucified and risen, are all there together.

20. Give Us This Bread Always

(From the Liturgy of the Word for the EIGHTEENTH SUNDAY OF THE YEAR) **B**

READING I   Ex 16:2-4, 12-15

A reading from the book of Exodus
I will rain bread from heaven upon you.

The whole Israelite community grumbled against Moses and Aaron. The Israelites said to them, "Would that we had died at the Lord's hand in the land of Egypt, as we sat by our fleshpots and ate our fill of bread! But you had to lead us into this desert to make the whole community die of famine!"

Then the Lord said to Moses, "I will now rain down bread from heaven for you. Each day the people are to go out and gather their daily portion; thus will I test them, to see whether they follow my instructions or not.

"I have heard the grumbling of the Israelites. Tell them: In the evening twilight you shall eat flesh, and in the morning you shall have your fill of bread, so that you may know that I, the Lord, am your God."

In the evening quail came up and covered the camp. In the morning a dew lay all about the camp, and when the dew evaporated, there on the surface of the desert were fine flakes like hoarfrost on the ground. On seeing it, the Israelites asked one another, "What is this?" for they did not know what it was. But Moses told them, "This is the bread which the Lord has given you to eat."

This is the Word of the Lord.

Responsorial Psalm   Ps 78:3-4, 23-24, 25, 54

R.   *(24) The Lord gave them bread from heaven.*

What we have heard and know,
    and what our fathers have declared to us,
We will declare to the generation to come the
        glorious deeds of the Lord and his strength
    and the wonders that he wrought.

R.   *The Lord gave them bread from heaven.*

He commanded the skies above
    and the doors of heaven he opened;
He rained manna upon them for food
    and gave them heavenly bread.

R.   *The Lord gave them bread from heaven.*

The bread of the mighty was eaten by men;
    even a surfeit of provisions he sent them.
And he brought them to his holy land,
    to the mountains his right hand had won.

R.   *The Lord gave them bread from heaven.*

READING II   Eph 4:17, 20-24

A reading from the letter of Paul to the Ephesians
Put on the new man that has been created in God's image.

I declare and solemnly attest in the Lord that you must no longer live as the pagans do—their minds empty. That is not what you learned when you learned Christ! I am supposing, of course, that he has been preached and taught to you in accord with the truth that is in Jesus: namely, that you must lay aside your former way of life and the old self which deteriorates through illusion and desire, and acquire a fresh, spiritual way of thinking. You must put on that new man created in God's image, whose justice and holiness are born of truth.

This is the Word of the Lord.

GOSPEL

Jn 6:24-35

Alleluia Jn 14:5

R.   *Alleluia.* I am the way, the truth, and the life, says the Lord;
   no one comes to the Father, except through me.

R.   *Alleluia.*

✠ *A reading from the holy gospel according to John*

He who comes to me will never be hungry; he who believes in me will never thirst.

When the crowd saw that neither Jesus nor his disciples were at the place where Jesus had eaten the bread, they too embarked in the boats and went to Capernaum looking for Jesus.

When they found him on the other side of the lake, they said to him, "Rabbi, when did you come here?" Jesus answered them:

"I assure you,
   you are not looking for me because you have seen signs
   but because you have eaten your fill of the loaves.
You should not be working for perishable food
   but for food that remains unto life eternal,
   food which the Son of Man will give you;
   it is on him that God the Father has set his seal."

At this they said to him, "What must we do to perform the works of God?" Jesus replied:

"This is the work of God:
   have faith in the One he sent."

"So that we can put faith in you," they asked him, "what sign are you going to perform for us to see? What is the 'work' you do? Our ancestors had manna to eat in the desert; according to Scripture, 'He gave them bread from the heavens to eat.' " Jesus said to them:

"I solemnly assure you,
   it was not Moses who gave you bread from the heavens;
   it is my Father who gives you the real heavenly bread.
God's bread comes down from heaven and
   gives life to the world."

"Sir, give us this bread always," they besought him.

Jesus explained to them:

"I myself am the bread of life.
No one who comes to me shall ever be hungry,
   no one who believes in me shall thirst again."

This is the gospel of the Lord.

21. Invitation to Supper

The priest then says quietly:

Priest: Lord Jesus Christ, Son of the living
God,
by the will of the Father and the work
of the Holy Spirit
your death brought life to the world.
By your holy body and blood
free me from all my sins and from every
evil.
Keep me faithful to your teaching,
and never let me be parted from you.

or

Lord Jesus Christ,
with faith in your love and mercy
I eat your body and drink your blood.
Let it not bring me condemnation,
but health in mind and body.

*Taking the host, raising it and facing
the people, he says:*

Priest: This is the Lamb of God
who takes away the sins of the world.
Happy are those who are called to his
supper.

All: *(Once only):*

Lord, I am not worthy to receive you,
but only say the word and I shall be
healed.

INVITATION TO THE LORD'S SUPPER

What shall we say when the Lord calls us to his supper? We came to celebrate with him and with each other that Jesus is the Lord. We have stood, waited, prayed, and gotten ourselves ready, singly and together, and now we are called to be happy together at his supper.

Spontaneously we answer: "Lord, I am not worthy . . . but . . ." But what? But, yes, of course, if you want me to. But, yes, of course, if you will say the word. The fact is he has already said the word: Come, come, do come. . . .

That's part of what makes us worthy even when we say we aren't. We aren't, but once we are called, we are worthy. The Lord's invitation has made us worthy. The call of the Lord is the only thing that makes us worthy.

We aren't worthy—except that we are. The less worthy we are, the more he wants us to come. We are worthy because out of love he created us. We are worthy because out of love he has died for us. "I came to save sinners," he said. Come you sinners. The bigger the sinner that is saved, the more God has done for him, the more he is worthy.

We aren't worthy—except that we are. We are his from the beginning, right down through the middle, and to the end of our lives because he has purchased us with his love and his life. We are even called his people. How could we be anybody else's? We are not on the outside looking in. We are on the inside, happy to be at home with him.

LORD, I AM NOT WORTHY

No one is worthy to stand before God. It is a fact that is quite obvious. The Lord just takes it for granted: "If you who are sinners know how to give your children good things . . ."

What is important is not our unworthiness (although it is essential that we acknowledge it) but our faith and confidence: "Only say the word and I shall be healed."

There was the centurion in Matthew's gospel whose servant was lying at home paralyzed, and in great pain. When Jesus said he would come and cure him, the centurion replied: "Sir, I am not worthy to have you under my roof; just give the word and my servant will be cured."

Matthew continues: "When Jesus heard this, he was astonished and said to those following him, 'I tell you solemnly, nowhere in Israel have I found faith like this.'"

When faith is strong it works wonders. When it's not there, St. James tells us in his epistle, we needn't expect anything. Not because God withholds his power from the unbelieving and untrusting, but because we need to trust and abandon ourselves. Only when we learn to rely no longer on our own strength and our own plans are we able to open ourselves to the power and guiding word of him in whom we believe.

Without faith, life ceases to have much meaning. With faith, we see wonders all around.

21. I Am the Living Bread

*(From the Liturgy of the Word for the
NINETEENTH SUNDAY OF THE YEAR)* **B**

READING I   **1 Kgs 19:4-8**

A reading from the first book of Kings
Strengthened by the food, he walked to the mountain
of the Lord.

Elijah went a day's jouney into the desert, until he came to a broom tree and sat beneath it. He prayed for death: "This is enough, O Lord! Take my life, for I am no better than my fathers." He lay down and fell asleep under the broom tree, but then an angel touched him and ordered him to get up and eat. He looked and there at his head was a hearth cake and a jug of water. After he ate and drank, he lay down again, but the angel of the Lord came back a second time, touched him, and ordered, "Get up and eat, else the journey will be too long for you!" He got up, ate and drank; then strengthened by that food, he walked forty days and forty nights to the mountain of God, Horeb.

This is the Word of the Lord.

Responsorial Psalm   **Ps 34:2-3, 4-5, 6-7, 8-9**

R.   *(9) Taste and see the goodness of the Lord.*

I will bless the Lord at all times;
    his praise shall be ever in my mouth.
Let my soul glory in the Lord;
    the lowly will hear me and be glad.

R.   *Taste and see the goodness of the Lord.*

Glorify the Lord with me,
    let us together extol his name.
I sought the Lord, and he answered me
    and delivered me from all my fears.

R.   *Taste and see the goodness of the Lord.*

Look to him that you may be radiant with joy,
    and your faces may not blush with shame.
When the afflicted man called out, the Lord heard,
    and from all his distress he saved him.

R.   *Taste and see the goodness of the Lord.*

The angel of the Lord encamps
    around those who fear him, and delivers them.
Taste and see how good the Lord is;
    happy the man who takes refuge in him.

R.   *Taste and see the goodness of the Lord.*

READING II   **Eph 4:30 - 5:2**

A reading from the letter of Paul to the Ephesians
Walk in love, just as Christ.

Do nothing to sadden the Holy Spirit with whom you were sealed against the day of redemption. Get rid of all bitterness, all passion and anger, harsh words, slander, and malice of every kind. In place of these, be kind to one another, compassionate, and mutually forgiving, just as God has forgiven you in Christ.

Be imitators of God as his dear children. Follow the way of love, even as Christ loved you. He gave himself for us as an offering to God, a gift of pleasing fragrance.

This is the Word of the Lord.

GOSPEL   Jn 6:41-51

Alleluia   Jn 14:23

R.   *Alleluia.* If anyone loves me, he will hold to
           my words,
        and my Father will love him, and we will
           come to him.
R.   *Alleluia.*

✠ *A reading from the holy gospel according to*
                    John
I am the living bread that came down from heaven.

The Jews started to murmur in protest because
Jesus claimed, "I am the bread that came down
from heaven." They kept saying: "Is this not
Jesus, the son of Joseph? Do we not know his
father and mother? How can he claim to have
come down from heaven?"
    "Stop your murmuring," Jesus told them.
    "No one can come to me
        unless the Father who sent me draws him;
        I will raise him up on the last day.

It is written in the prophets:
    'They shall all be taught by God.'
Everyone who has heard the Father
    and learned from him
    comes to me.
Not that anyone has seen the Father—
    only the one who is from God
    has seen the Father.
Let me firmly assure you,
    he who believes has eternal life.
I am the bread of life.
Your ancestors ate manna in the desert, but
        they died.
This is the bread that comes down from
        heaven,
    for a man to eat and never die.
I myself am the living bread
    come down from heaven.
If anyone eats this bread
    he shall live forever;
    the bread I will give
    is my flesh, for the life of the world."

        This is the gospel of the Lord.

22. The Meal Together

When giving Communion the priest says:

Priest: The body of Christ.
People: Amen.

To the prayer after communion the people respond:

People: Amen.

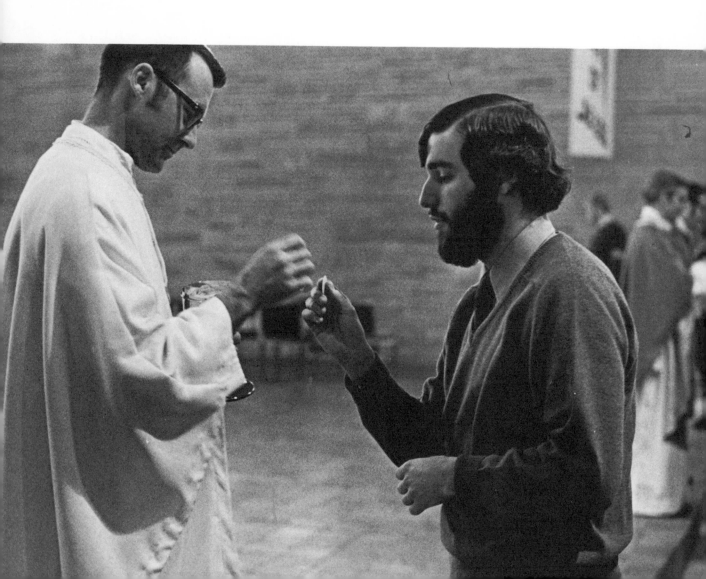

COMMUNION

To the Father:

Father, your kindness is beyond words:

You have gathered us together in Jesus
You have forgiven us in his name

> We have reconciled ourselves to our brothers
> So we may ourselves be forgiven

"You have fed us with your Word
Now you feed us with your Son:

> Bread to share with one another
> Wine to gladden our hearts together."
> *(Eucharistic Liturgies)*

To the Son:

Your memory we keep, O Lord

Especially those last moments
When you spoke with such loving urgency:

> Do not let your hearts be troubled . . .
> I shall not be with you much longer . . .
> My commandment is that you love one another . . .

> I shall not call you servants any more
> I shall call you friends
> You are my friends,
> If you do what I command you

> A man can have no greater love
> Than to lay down his life for his friends

You have been lifted up, O Lord
Now draw all things to yourself.

To the Holy Spirit:

Now we know how good it is that Jesus went
    away
> For we have his Spirit of love among us

> Who makes us cry "Abba, Father"
> Who teaches us in our hearts
> Who breathes into us new life
> Who makes us springs of "living water"
> To live as a people in peace and love

Indeed, he did not leave us orphans
Come, O Holy Spirit, Come!

HOW I HAVE LONGED!

"With desire have I desired to eat this pasch with you. . . ."

"I have greatly desired to eat this passover with you. . . ."

"I have longed to eat this passover. . . ."

"How I have longed. . . . !"

"I have longed and longed to share this paschal meal with you. . . ."

These are the words of Jesus, variously translated, as he sat down with his apostles to his last supper with them.

This was no ordinary meal for Jesus. This is no ordinary meal for us.

For Jesus it was the meal before he suffered, before he died. For Jesus it was the meal he had waited for to share with his friends, it was the meal on which he would heap special significance, special love, special power. It was the meal that would never end.

It is meant to be the same for us: strength before we go out and suffer for others, a meal steeped in significance, a meal shared with friends, a meal marking our identity with Jesus, a meal binding the Christ in all of us together into communion and community.

The bread is our sign. "The body of Christ," the priest says.

And each of us says "Amen" to that, knowing that the bread is the sign of the body given to us for our life together.

Let anyone who can say "Amen" to the bread and to "the body of Christ" come forward now, eat and be friends, be happy, be joyful, be healed, be grateful, be warm with love and celebrate in his heart.

127

22. My Flesh Is Real Food

(From the Liturgy of the Word for the
TWENTIETH SUNDAY OF THE YEAR)   **B**

READING I   **Prv 9:1-6**

A reading from the book of Proverbs
Come and eat my bread, drink the wine I have prepared.

Wisdom has built her house,
  she has set up her seven columns;
She has dressed her meat, mixed her wine,
  yes, she has spread her table.
She has sent out her maidens; she calls
  from the heights out over the city:
"Let whoever is simple turn in here;
  to him who lacks understanding, I say,
Come, eat of my food,
  and drink of the wine I have mixed!
Forsake foolishness that you may live;
  advance in the way of understanding.

> This is the Word of the Lord.

Responsorial Psalm Ps 34:2-3, 10-11, 12-13, 14-15

R. (9) Taste and see the goodness of the Lord.

I will bless the Lord at all times;
  his praise shall be ever in my mouth.
Let my soul glory in the Lord;
  the lowly will hear me and be glad.

R. Taste and see the goodness of the Lord.

Fear the Lord, you his holy ones,
  for nought is lacking to those who fear him.
The great grow poor and hungry;
  but those who seek the Lord want for no good
     thing.

R. Taste and see the goodness of the Lord.

Come, children, hear me;
  I will teach you the fear of the Lord.
Which of you desires life,
  and takes delight in prosperous days?

R. Taste and see the goodness of the Lord.

Keep your tongue from evil
  and your lips from speaking guile;
Turn from evil, and do good;
  seek peace, and follow after it.

R. Taste and see the goodness of the Lord.

READING II   **Eph 5:15-20**

A reading from the letter of Paul to the Ephesians
Be watchful that you may know the will of God.

Keep careful watch over your conduct. Do not act like fools, but like thoughtful men. Make the most of the present opportunity, for these are evil days. Do not continue in ignorance, but try to discern the will of the Lord. Avoid getting drunk on wine that leads to debauchery. Be filled with the Spirit, addressing one another in psalms and hymns and inspired songs. Sing praise to the Lord with all your hearts. Give thanks to God the Father always and for everything in the name of our Lord Jesus Christ.

> This is the Word of the Lord.

GOSPEL   **Jn 6:51-58**

Alleluia   Jn 6:64, 69

R.   *Alleluia.* Your words, O Lord, are spirit and
        life,
        you have the words of everlasting life.

R.   *Alleluia.*

✠ *A reading from the holy gospel according to*
                    John
My flesh is real food and my blood is real drink.

Jesus said to the crowds:
  "I myself am the living bread
     come down from heaven.
  If anyone eats this bread
     he shall live forever;
     the bread I will give
     is my flesh, for the life of the world."
At this the Jews quarreled among themselves,
saying, "How can he give us his flesh to eat?"
Thereupon Jesus said to them:
  "Let me solemnly assure you,
     if you do not eat the flesh of the Son of Man
     and drink his blood,
     you have no life in you.
  He who feeds on my flesh
     and drinks my blood
     has life eternal,
     and I will raise him up on the last day.
  For my flesh is real food
     and my blood real drink.
  The man who feeds on my flesh
     and drinks my blood
     remains in me, and I in him.
  Just as the Father who has life sent me
     and I have life because of the Father,
     so the man who feeds on me
     will have life because of me.

This is the bread that came down from heaven.
Unlike your ancestors who ate and died none-
     theless,
  the man who feeds on this bread shall live
     forever."

GOSPEL (21st Sunday)   **Jn 6:60-69**

Lord, whom shall we go to? You have the words
of eternal life.

Many of the disciples of Jesus remarked, "This
sort of talk is hard to endure! How can anyone
take it seriously?" Jesus was fully aware that his
disciples were murmuring in protest at what he
had said. "Does it shake your faith?" he asked
them.
  "What, then, if you were to see the Son of Man
     ascend to where he was before . . . ?
  It is the spirit that gives life;
     the flesh is useless.
  The words I spoke to you
     are spirit and life.
  Yet among you there are some who do not
     believe."
(Jesus knew from the start, of course, the ones
who refused to believe, and the one who would
hand him over.) He went on to say:
  "This is why I have told you
     that no one can come to me
     unless it is granted him by the Father."
From this time on, many of his disciples broke
away and would not remain in his company any
longer. Jesus then said to the Twelve, "Do you
want to leave me too?" Simon Peter answered
him, "Lord, to whom shall we go? You have the
words of eternal life. We have come to believe;
we are convinced that you are God's holy one."

This is the gospel of the Lord.

I saw a new heaven and a new earth and i saw the NEW CITY coming from God out of heaven

PART 5

Concluding Rite

23. The Blessing

Priest: The Lord be with you.
People: And also with you.

Priest: May almighty God bless you, the Father
and the Son, and the Holy Spirit.
People: Amen.

BLESSINGS IN THE BIBLE

We read early in the bible that when God first created man and woman, he blessed them.

God blessed Abraham when he sent him into a new country. Moreover, God promised to bless them that Abraham would bless.

In a significant event, Melchisedech, "priest of the most high God," brought out bread and wine and blessed Abraham en route on his journey.

Abraham blessed Isaac, and Isaac blessed Jacob, and Jacob blessed his sons.

In a very strange story, Jacob, on leaving Laban and preparing to meet Esau, wrestled all night with an "angel," and even though his hip was dislocated in the struggle, he would not let go of the "angel" until he had wrested a blessing from God.

Tobias blessed the marriage of his son to Sarah in the phrase still used: "The God of Abraham, the God of Isaac, and the God of Jacob be with you."

Jesus blessed the loaves and fishes that he multiplied for the crowd.

When the little children came to him, Jesus put his arms around them and blessed them before they went away again.

At the last supper Jesus blessed the bread and wine, the night before he died, leaving it for a sign of himself after his going away.

In a final gesture of love, Jesus lifted up his hands and blessed his disciples as he departed from them at the ascension.

All these blessings were occasioned by situations involving departures of one kind or another.

THE BLESSING

The blessing is a good-bye, a word which comes to us from "God be with you."

It is a most common thing among us to part with a blessing in our hearts for one another, and in our hearts we know that all blessings come from God. To bless is to believe in God.

While all blessings do, indeed, come from God, we are God's instruments in blessing—the people of God in a special way, and among the people of God the priest in a still more special way. All who are baptized into the priesthood of Christ, and all who believe in God, are his instruments of blessing.

That priests bless the people in God's name, and that parents ask the blessing of God on their children have a long history and precedent in the bible.

That Christians bless one another and all the world is the message of Jesus. We are sent on our way with the blessing of God to bring the good news to all men that in Jesus we are all blessed.

23. The Multitude of the Blessed

(From the Liturgy of the Word for November 1, ALL SAINTS)

READING I   Rv 7:2-4, 9-14

A reading from the book of Revelation
I saw an immense crowd, beyond hope of counting, of people from every nation, race, tribe and language.

I, John, saw another angel come up from the east holding the seal of the living God. He cried out at the top of his voice to the four angels who were given power to ravage the land and the sea, "Do no harm to the land or the sea or the trees until we imprint this seal on the foreheads of the servants of our God." I heard the number of those who were so marked—one hundred and forty-four thousand from every tribe of Israel.

After this I saw before me a huge crowd which no one could count from every nation, race, people, and tongue. They stood before the throne and the Lamb, dressed in long white robes and holding palm branches in their hands. They cried out in a loud voice, "Salvation is from our God, who is seated on the throne, and from the Lamb!" All the angels who were standing around the throne and the elders and the four living creatures fell down before the throne to worship God. They said: "Amen! Praise and glory, wisdom, thanksgiving, and honor, power and might to our God forever and ever. Amen!"

Then one of the elders asked me, "Who do you think these are, all dressed in white? And where have they come from?" I said to him, "Sir, you should know better than I." He then told me, "These are the ones who have survived the great period of trial; they have washed their robes and made them white in the blood of the Lamb."

This is the Word of the Lord.

Responsorial Psalm   Ps 24:1-2, 3-4, 5-6

R. *(6) Lord, this is the people that longs to see your face.*

The Lord's are the earth and its fullness;
    the world and those who dwell in it.
For he founded it upon the seas
    and established it upon the rivers.

R. *Lord, this is the people that longs to see your face.*

Who can ascend the mountain of the Lord?
    or who may stand in his holy place?
He whose hands are sinless, whose heart is clean,
    who desires not what is vain.

R. *Lord, this is the people that longs to see your face.*

He shall receive a blessing from the Lord,
    a reward from God his savior.
Such is the race that seeks for him,
    that seeks the face of the God of Jacob.

R. *Lord, this is the people that longs to see your face.*

A reading from the first letter of John
We shall see God as he really is.

See what love the Father has bestowed on us
    in letting us be called children of God!
Yet that in fact is what we are.
The reason the world does not recognize us
    is that it never recognized the Son.
Dearly beloved,
    we are God's children now;
    what we shall later be has not yet come to
        light.
We know that when it comes to light
    we shall be like him,
    for we shall see him as he is.
Everyone who has this hope based on him
    keeps himself pure, as he is pure.

This is the Word of the Lord.

Alleluia Mt 11:28

R.   *Alleluia.* Come to me, all you that labor and
         are burdened,
      and I will give you rest, says the Lord.
R.   *Alleluia.*

✠ *A reading from the holy gospel according to*
Matthew
Rejoice and be glad for your reward will be great in heaven.

When Jesus saw the crowds he went up on the
mountainside. After he had sat down his disciples
gathered around him, and he began to teach
them:
    "How blest are the poor in spirit: the reign of
        God is theirs.
    Blest too are the sorrowing; they shall be con-
        soled.
    [Blest are the lowly; they shall inherit the land.]
    Blest are they who hunger and thirst for holi-
        ness;
      they shall have their fill.
    Blest are they who show mercy; mercy shall be
        theirs.
    Blest are the single-hearted, for they shall see
        God.
    Blest too the peacemakers; they shall be called
        sons of God.
    Blest are those persecuted for holiness' sake;
        the reign of God is theirs.
    Blest are you when they insult you and perse-
        cute you and utter every kind of slander
        against you because of me.
    Be glad and rejoice, for your reward in heaven
        is great."

This is the gospel of the Lord.

24. Go . . .

Priest: Go in the peace of Christ.

or

The Mass is ended, go in peace.

or

Go in peace to love and serve the Lord.

People: Thanks be to God.

LIVE THE MASS

Our service is not finished with a few gestures.

The Mass is a sign and a revelation of what is actually taking place in our own lives and in the life of the community, or it may be only an empty gourd or a clashing cymbal.

We have heard God's Word and eaten the Bread of Life. Now it is time for us to leave, to do good, to praise and bless the Lord in our daily lives.

It is easy enough to say; we have heard it hundreds of times. Do we allow its full meaning to penetrate our consciousness?

As one spiritual writer put it: In the Mass we have seen God at work in human life, a God who loves us so much that he took thousands of years to break gently into the life of the world, and finally actually become a man to be among us. He became a servant, humble, gentle, poor, with the good news that our God is a God who loves, who forgives, who is everlastingly concerned for our welfare.

At Mass we are summoned and commissioned to continue that revelation of God's loving action in the lives of men and the world by repeating his gestures of love, sharing, forgiving.

We have no better place to start than in our own homes, among the members of our own families.

Every time we share a meal, then, give thanks, recall God's mercies, forgive each other's faults, we carry on the Eucharist, the Mass, where we remember and imitate him who chose to love us "even to the death on the cross."

That is the burden and the privilege we bear.

GO . . .

We are leaving. We are leaving the place made sacred by our coming together for worship, made sacred by being set aside as the ritual meeting place of man with the mystery of God, a special place for rendezvous between God and man.

Almost everything we did there, and said there, was a sign—from putting our host in to sharing Christ's body in communion—a sacred sign putting us in touch with a world which we cannot touch and see, a world more important than the world we can lay our hands on.

The world of God is world of mystery and world of spirit. What is most human about us is spirit and mystery; what we seek to become and what we yearn for in our deepest heart is hidden and invisible.

The whole effort, activity, and significance of what mankind calls religion is to make contact and keep contact with the mystery of God, with the Spirit of love which is at the heart of the human in man.

We are leaving, but we are not *just* leaving. We are being sent away, out of this sacred place into the world, in which, if Jesus' coming to us means anything, it means our going out as he did to express the mystery of God and to keep alive the Spirit of love among ourselves and among others in the world.

24. The Second Coming

(From the Liturgy of the Word for the
THIRTY-FOURTH OR LAST SUNDAY
OF THE YEAR, CHRIST THE KING)

A

READING I   Ez 34:11-12, 15-17

A reading from the book of the prophet Ezekiel
You, my flock, I judge between sheep and sheep, between
rams and he-goats.

Thus says the Lord God: I myself will look after
and tend my sheep. As a shepherd tends his flock
when he finds himself among his scattered sheep,
so will I tend my sheep. I will rescue them from
every place where they were scattered when it
was cloudy and dark. I myself will pasture my
sheep; I myself will give them rest, says the Lord
God. The lost I will seek out, the strayed I will
bring back, the injured I will bind up, the sick
I will heal [but the sleek and the strong I will
destroy], shepherding them rightly.

As for you, my sheep, says the Lord God, I
will judge between one sheep and another, between rams and goats.

This is the Word of the Lord.

Responsorial Psalm   Ps 23:1-2, 2-3, 5-6

R.   *(1) The Lord is my shepherd; there is noth-*
        ing I shall want.

The Lord is my shepherd; I shall not want.
    In verdant pastures he gives me repose.

R.   *The Lord is my shepherd; there is nothing*
        I shall want.

Beside restful waters he leads me;
    he refreshes my soul.
He guides me in right paths
    for his name's sake.

R.   *The Lord is my shepherd; there is nothing*
        I shall want.

You spread the table before me
    in the sight of my foes;
You anoint my head with oil;
    my cup overflows.
Only goodness and kindness follow me
    all the days of my life;
And I shall dwell in the house of the Lord
    for years to come.

R.   *The Lord is my shepherd; there is nothing*
        I shall want.

READING II
1 Cor 15:20-26, 28

A reading from the first letter of Paul to the Corinthians

He will hand over the kingdom to God the Father, so that God may be all in all.

Christ has been raised from the dead, the first fruits of those who have fallen asleep. Death came through a man; hence the resurrection of the dead comes through a man also. Just as in Adam all die, so in Christ all will come to life again, but each one in proper order: Christ the first-fruits and then, at his coming, all those who belong to him. After that will come the end, when, after having destroyed every sovereignty, authority, and power, he will hand over the kingdom to God the Father. Christ must reign until God has put all enemies under his feet, and the last enemy to be destroyed is death. When, finally, all has been subjected to the Son, he will then subject himself to the One who made all things subject to him, so that God may be all in all.

This is the Word of the Lord.

GOSPEL
Mt 25:31-46

Alleluia   Mk 11:10

R.   *Alleluia.* Blessed is he who inherits the kingdom of David our father;

blessed is he who comes in the name of the Lord.

R.   *Alleluia.*

✛ *A reading from the holy gospel according to Matthew*

He will sit upon his seat of glory and he will separate men one from another.

Jesus said to his disciples: "When the Son of Man comes in his glory, escorted by all the angels of heaven, he will sit upon his royal throne, and all the nations will be assembled before him. Then he will separate them into two groups, as a shepherd separates sheep from goats. The sheep he will place on his right hand, the goats on his left. The king will say to those on his right: 'Come. You have my Father's blessing! Inherit the kingdom prepared for you from the creation of the world. For I was hungry and you gave me food, I was thirsty and you gave me drink. I was a stranger and you welcomed me, naked and you clothed me. I was ill and you comforted me, in prison and you came to visit me.' Then the just will ask him: 'Lord, when did we see you hungry and feed you or see you thirsty and give you drink? When did we welcome you away from home or clothe you in your nakedness? When did we visit you when you were ill or in prison?' The king will answer them: 'I assure you, as often as you did it for one of my least brothers, you did it for me.'

"Then he will say to those on his left: 'Out of my sight, you condemned, into that everlasting fire prepared for the devil and his angels! I was hungry and you gave me no food, I was thirsty and you gave me no drink. I was away from home and you gave me no welcome, naked and you gave me no clothing. I was ill and in prison and you did not come to comfort me.' Then they in turn will ask: 'Lord, when did we see you hungry or thirsty or away from home or naked or ill or in prison and not attend you in your needs?' He will answer them: 'I assure you, as often as you neglected to do it to one of these least ones, you neglected to do it to me.' These will go off to eternal punishment and the just to eternal life."

This is the gospel of the Lord.

140